The 3 Reasons Why Book of Lifestyle

Inspire. Educate. Entertain.

By 3RW & Ryan Stabile

www.3reasonswhy.com

See more reasons for everything at:

www.3ReasonsWhy.com

The 3 Reasons Why Book of Lifestyle

First Edition.

Dedication

For all of those who seek knowledge.

Table of Contents

Introduction

The human race and our insatiable pursuit of knowledge is a tale that begins at the dawn of time. For better or for worse, seeking out knowledge is hardwired into the human brain.

In fact, our quest for knowledge has historically often gotten the human race into trouble from the very beginning. Whether it be partaking in the forbidden fruit or the inquisitive cavemen of the prehistoric period who had to *know* which dinosaurs were herbivores and which were carnivores through a fatal series of trial and errors, knowing and not know can sometimes mean the difference between life and death.

Yet, still, the human race persists in *knowing things.*

Once our ancestors had their food, shelter and basic survival necessities fulfilled, they had the luxury of kicking back to relax as they ponder the mysteries of the universe.

The human race's biggest nemesis on their quest for knowledge has always been that daunting three letter word: why?

Everywhere you look, there is a potential "why?". While it would be difficult to go through life and ponder "why?" at every turn, sometimes you need to just kick back, relax and ask yourself all of those little questions. Only by asking the questions will you find the reasons for "why?". Those reasons are the only way that the human race can grow, learn and evolve beyond a prehistoric caveman. Because the more you know, the more you grow.

At 3RW, we believe that there are no stupid questions, only superfluous answers. A thirst for knowledge should not be oversaturated, like the constant barrage of information on the internet, or teased with just a few droplets of wisdom that only serve to intensify your thirst. 3 reasons are all you need to answer any "why?" and *The 3 Reasons Why Book of Lifestyle* is your secret weapon in the fight against "why?".

Find out more of the 3 reasons behind life's biggest and littlest mysteries at the world's largest source for knowledge, www.3ReasonsWhy.com.

LIFESTYLE

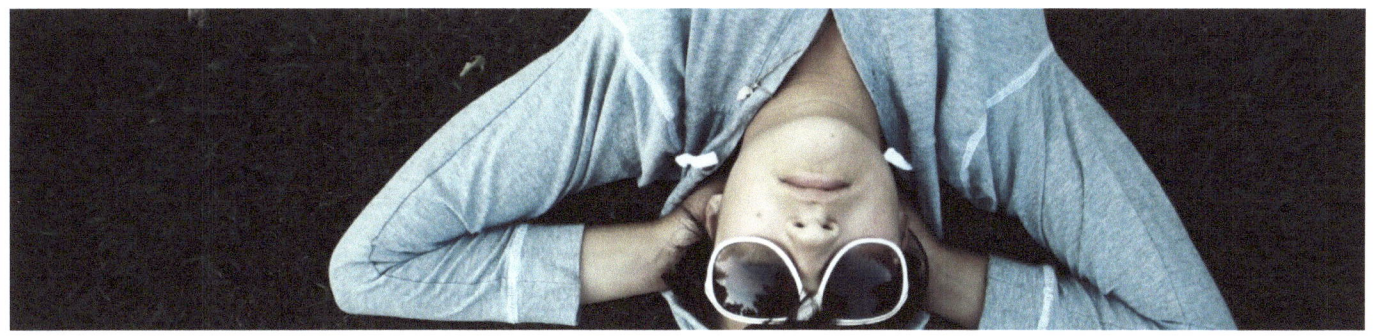

3 Reasons Why we get bored

Even the most interesting man in the world inevitably will become bored at some stage in his life. No one likes being bored, especially in the company of other. Like many terminal illnesses, once we understand why we get bored we will be able to prevent it in the future.

Here are three reasons why we get bored.

Reason 1: Uninteresting Facts

Boredom is defined as "an aversive state of wanting, but being unable, to engage in satisfying activity, which springs from failures in one of the brain's attention networks." As defined by psychological scientist John Eastwood of York University in Ontario, Canada. German psychologist Theodor Lipps, however, proposed one of the earliest definitions of boredom in 1903, saying, "Boredom is a feeling of displeasure arising out of a conflict between a need for intense mental activity and lack of incitement to it, or inability to be incited." So, are you bored yet?

Reason 2: Environmental Stimuli

Attention and environmental awareness are the keys to boredom, or lack thereof. When we have difficulty paying attention to our environment, we become bored easily. If we find ourselves in an environment with little to no stimuli, or a "boring" place, then there is no reason for us to mentally pay attention. When there is no reason for us to pay attention to something, we become bored. Even if you realize that you need to pay attention to a particular lecture in class or risk failing the course, it will not prevent that material from being boring.

Reason 3: Danger, Sex & Comedy

What if I told you that you have been poisoned, and the only way to find the antidote is by carefully reading this entire article? The key to attention is a peripheral sense of danger. When our mind' sense that danger is near, we enter a heightened state of awareness. But that's not all that prevents us from being bored.

Other forms of entertainment which engage our sense and prevent us from being bored are activities which trigger relaxing Beta wavelengths in the mind. In particular, anything we find funny or sexually arousing will prevent us from being bored.

Now that we better understand the three reasons why we become bored, it will be easier to prevent terminal boredom in the future. By engaging our senses with anything dangerous, hilarious, or sexual, we are able to keep our senses alert and aware, preventing boredom.

3 Reasons Why men go bald

Although baldness occurs in women as well, it is much more prominent in men. Through this article, we will explain the three most common reasons why men lose their hair and explore ways in which you may be able to prevent future hair loss.

Here are three reasons why men go bald.

Reason 1: Genetics

You've probably often heard it said the genetics is the number one leading cause of hair loss for both men and women. While there is no specific "baldness gene", if you come from a line of men who have suffered from hair loss, then you are more likely to lose your hair at an early age. Additionally, every white male will get some type of baldness at some stage in his life. Your chance of becoming bald later in life increases along with the number of first and second degree relatives who are also bald.

Reason 2: Age

As time passes, the tiny cavities known as hair follicles at the base of your scalp shrink as hair thinks and thins. This happens in all men as they age, although some more premature than others. Eventually, hair follicles simply stop producing new strands of hair. Certain hair products may help prolong the effects of balding, however, losing your hair in simply a natural part of aging. Based on research studies, it is estimated that 30% of men have male pattern baldness at age 30 and 50% of men by age 50.

Reason 3: Hormones

Hormones are also a huge contributing factor to baldness, which is the primary reason that men are much more likely to go bald long before women. Men with hormone deficiencies will lose their hair much quicker. Interestingly enough, men who have been castrated do not suffer from hair loss, so if you want to keep the hair you have, the solution is to lose another part of body.

While all of these factors individually contribute to male pattern baldness and the gradual shrinkage of their hair follicles, it is a combination of all of them that leads to hair loss. As we can see from these three reasons, for many men, becoming bald is simply a part of getting older and is often easier to embrace rather than fight it.

3 Reasons Why Microadventures is becoming more popular

In today's world, who can really afford to take those long, expensive vacations to exotic locations for weeks at a time? instead, what we are seeing more and more often is the emergence of micro-adventures, or day-trips to local exotic location, which provide much needed refreshment and replenishing one's mental fortitude without the downtime of being away from work for weeks at a time.

Here are three reasons why micro-adventures are becoming more popular.

Reason 1: Refresh

In order to not get burnt out at our day jobs, everyone requires a little micro-adventure now and again. While some require a bit more training and preparation, such as climbing Mount Kilimanjaro, others are a simple nice retreat, such as cliff jumping into the Colorado River. In either case, micro-adventures provide a refreshing thrill of adventure for people who can't be away from work for extended periods of time.

Reason 2: They're family friendly

Think micro-adventures are just for big short CEOs? Think again. There are many micro-adventure packages available for more family-oriented outings, such as a hike to an excellent picnic spot or a day of swimming at a local lake. These micro-adventures are also significantly less expensive than traditional vacation packages and can sometimes cost less than $100 a day, as opposed to $1,000 or more for a 3-day weekend vacation.

Reason 3: Getting back to nature

Especially for those working in big cities, it's important to get back to nature now and again in order to refresh the mind. The three secret ingredients which make up an excellent micro-adventure are sea, sun, and sand. If you work out in the middle of nature, you may want to plan a day trip into the city full of sightseeing and other events for your next micro-adventure – anything to break free from the norm!

As we can see from the above reasons, there are many benefits to taking micro-adventures as opposed to traditional, longer vacations. As if you need any more of an excuse to go take your next vacation, start planning your micro-adventure today and explore the local scenery around your town!

3 Reasons why Going Out On Your Own can be transformative

Whether you just moved to a new place, are traveling alone, or are looking to meet some friendly locals, going out on your own can be a transformative process on the road to personal growth.

Here are three reasons why going out on your own can be transformative.

Reason 1: Personal growth

When you make the active decision to go out on your own, it can be transformative. Taking the first steps to growing yourself on a personal level can be difficult, but if you are committed, you will gain tools which will stick with you for the rest of your life. When you first start going out on your own, don't expect the best results right away. This type of personal growth is an incremental journey, one which will take a while to get used to and master.

Reason 2: A social monster

Making new friends is tough, especially when we, as a society, are conditioned to stick to our small group of close-knit friends we've had for years. It takes an empathetic type of social monster to walk into a bar or restaurant and say hello to the first group of people you see, but you really set the tone for the entire night when you do that. This is the first step to empowering yourself on your journey to transformative personal growth.

Reason 3: Satisfied with your life

People may go out on their own for many different reasons, one of which is that we may have moved to a new place recently and are looking to make some new friends. If you are unsatisfied with your current life and set of friends or people you surround yourself with, you may be looking for a transformative new beginning, and going out on your own is surely the right path. Your life will also be transformed by changing the people with whom you surround yourself. When meeting new people, ask yourself, "Is this the type of person I want to build a life-long friendship or relationship with?" If the person has a positive attitude or will bring a transformative sense of positivity into your life, then the answer is likely an overwhelming yes!

As we can see, there are many reasons for going out all by yourself. You may want to meet new friends or are looking to develop your own personal growth, but any way you look at it, going out on your own can be a transformative process.

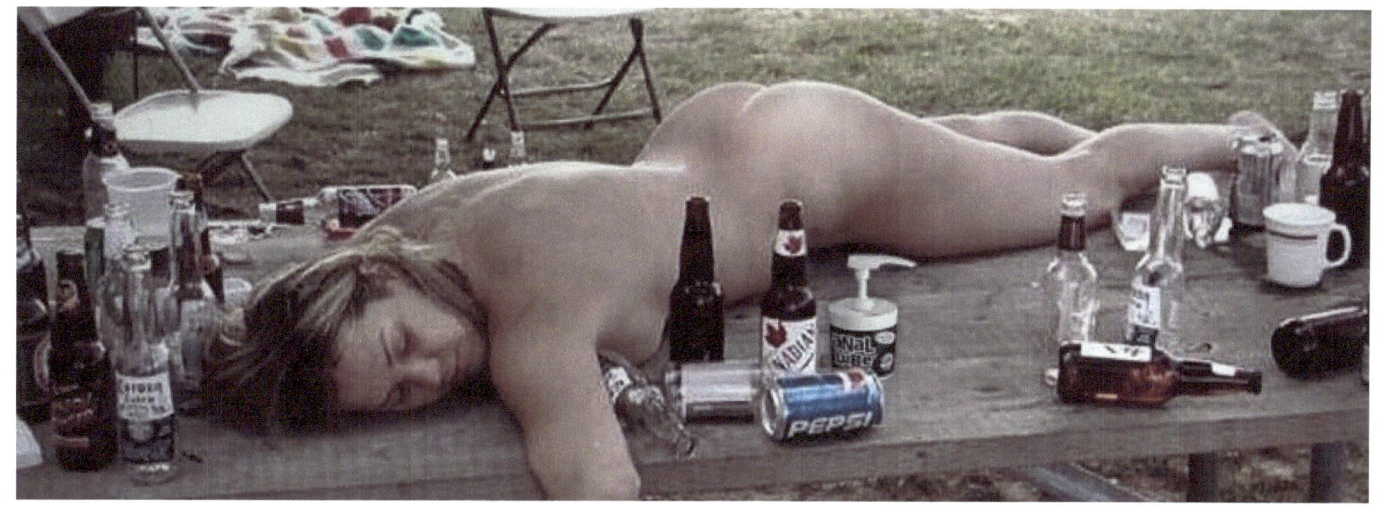

3 Reasons Why we suffer from hangovers and what to do about it

Alcohol is bad, m'kay? After a night of hard drinking and partying, chances are, you'll wake up feeling like less than your best. With a myriad of hangover cures out there, it's important to understand what is going on in your body and how to prevent or best remedy hangovers.

Here are three reasons why we suffer from a hangover and what to do about it.

Reason 1: Hangovers – know your enemy

Fatigue, dry mouth and headaches are both symptoms of a hangover, but the biggest sign that you might have a hangover is the fact that you were out all night drinking. These all set in only hours after your last bring, which is why you might have the compulsion to grab another one – instead, start the mending process and reach for a glass of water.

Reason 2: Congeners – know your alcohol

Congeners are the chemical byproduct in darker alcohols, such as whiskey, bourbon, dark beers and red wine. These congeners are what cause hangovers, although they can even be found in white wine and clear liquors as well. A 2009 study found that people who drank bourbon, which contains 37 times more congeners than vodka, suffered exponentially worse hangovers than people swilling the clear stuff. As a reminder, choose your alcohol wisely!

Reason 3: Remedies – know your cures

It is a question as old as time itself – what is the best cure for a hangover? More alcohol is almost always a bad idea and only prolongs and even bigger hangover on the horizon. The best remedies are also the obvious ones – lots and lots of water, greasy food, and asprin. Alcohol is a diuretic, which is also why we pee so much when we drink beer. One of the time tested methods of preventing a hangover while you're out drinking is to punctuate every alcoholic drink you have with a glass of water. By replacing water with the alcohol we drink, we prevent ourselves from becoming overly dehydrated and a resulting hangover the following morning.

3 Reasons Why we fidget when trying to fall asleep

Fidgeting is a process wherein one couldn't sit still. When you're someone who's fidgety, you tend to move a lot in your seat, move your hand and feet, and is always moving about. In some cases, many individuals fidget when they are trying to sleep at night.

Here are the reasons why we fidget when trying to fall asleep.

Reason 1: Discomfort

It could be the bed, the linens, or the whole ambience that make you feel uncomfortable and cause you to fidget when you're about to take your much needed rest. Discomfort is one of the reasons why you can't doze off to dreamland right away. For example, there are those who prefer using a particular pillow, one they're accustomed to. Once they sleep without such pillow, they feel different and uncomfortable. The same thing goes when you're used to sleeping in your own bed which you have for several years and suddenly you have no choice but to sleep in a hotel or dorm using a different bed. Such discomforts can cause you to fidget until your eyes are too heavy you can barely keep them open.

Reason 2: Anxiety

It is only normal to feel anxious once in a while especially when you have to deal with so many problems such as your finances or job. People who worry too much often fidget before falling into a deep sleep. That's because they keep wondering what will happen next, how will they solve their problems, or what awaits them tomorrow. People who suffer from anxiety don't only fidget but also prone to having difficulty in getting themselves to sleep.

Reason 3: Too much caffeine

Sometimes, drinking too much coffee is also to blame for fidgeting before going to sleep. Caffeine is a stimulant and drinking too much can make you stay awake the whole night. Too much caffeine can cause irritability which is why you move a lot or fidget before you are finally able to fall asleep.

There's nothing to worry about if you often fidget before going to sleep. It could be that you're only uncomfortable or anxious. Another reason is that you consumed too much caffeine for the day.

3 Reasons Why yawning is so contagious

Have you ever noticed that when someone yawns, you yourself feel the unstoppable desire to yawn as well? Why is this? Is it magic? Do you have no control over your bodily functions? Surely yawning indicates tiredness, doesn't it? So why do people irresistibly feel that they have to yawn once someone else has?

Here are 3 reasons why yawning is so contagious.

Reason 1: Tiredness and empathy

Apparently, only about half of people do yawn after someone else has. It was always presumed that the contagiousness of the yawn was down to things like tiredness, empathy and energy levels, but recently this has been thrown into some dispute. More than anything, it seems to come down to the individual. Some people are more susceptible to contagious yawning than others. In fact, scientists have found that some people will yawn just by reading the word yawn!

Reason 2: Age

Only humans and chimpanzees are susceptible to contagious yawning, so there's definitely something that sets us apart from the rest of the animal kingdom in this respect. Scientists have performed lots of studies to find out why we yawn. They have discovered that it has little to do with empathy, intelligence or the time of day, but they have identified that age may be an important factor, although this evidence is not conclusive.

Reason 3: Genetic makeup

Genetic influences may have a lot to do with why we yawn after seeing or hearing someone else yawn, but this is an area that needs to be studied a lot more before any firm conclusions can be arrived at.

So, we still don't know for certain! Anyway, with all this talk of yawning, it's very likely that many of you will have already started stretching your arms above your heads and have started to perform the yawning act; or maybe you are trying to hold a yawn in! Go on- have a big yawn!

3 Reasons Why we suffer from motion sickness

Why is it that some people have sea-legs and will feel quite comfortable navigating their way across the choppy ocean whilst some people will feel queasier than a man on a rollercoaster who's just eaten an oyster supper followed by cream donuts? Of course, it's not only being on a boat that can cause motion sickness. Plenty of buses, cars and – yes - rollercoasters also have the effect on many people. Are you interested to know why this is?

Here are three reasons why we suffer from motion sickness

Reason 1: Sensory disagreements

Motion sickness is also known as kinetosis. The condition comes about as result of a disagreement between the movement you can see with your own eyes and the vestibular system's sense of movement. The vestibular system is our sensory system that gives the sense of balance and spatial awareness. So when these two forms of sensory perception are opposed to one another, from the action of being in an airplane or a coach (for example), it's easy to see where that feeling of nausea comes from. Motion sickness can also make you feel fatigue and dizziness. Other symptoms include: pale skin, a cold sweat, vomiting, an increase in saliva, rapid breathing, drowsiness and headaches.

Reason 2: Some are more likely to suffer than others

Some people are more prone to motion sickness than others. For instance, women during periods and pregnancy are more vulnerable to it. People who often get migraines are also likely to experience motion sickness.

Reason 3: Motion sickness is common in children

In children aged 3-12, motion sickness is very common. Children usually grow out of it in their teenage years. If you suffer from motion sickness, or if your children do, be prepared! Most importantly, make sure you have motion sickness tablets from your pharmacist or doctor; if you don't want to be spending your journey in an awful state, that is.

3 Reasons Why people get addicted to coffee

Do you drink coffee? Do you drink a lot of coffee? Do you drink too much coffee? Plenty of people may well answer yes. With it being such an everyday stimulant, it's easy to overlook just how addictive it can be. So why do people get addicted to coffee?

Here are 3 reasons why people get addicted to coffee.

Reason 1: It helps!

Coffee helps you wake up in the morning. It also helps you get to work and function for the rest of the day. For many, this is exactly how things are. Coffee can certainly help to keep you sharp, but as with any stimulant, it's all about balance and moderation. Don't let the morning kick you require become an all-out addiction.

Reason 2: What's going on in the brain

So, coffee helps you get through the day, but what's going on biologically and why is it so addictive? It all has to do with how the drug affects the brain. When you ingest caffeine, the substance is absorbed through the small intestine before dissolving into the bloodstream. The chemical can be dissolved by both water-based solutions, like water, and fat-based ones, like cell membranes. Because of this, it is able to enter the brain. The structure of caffeine is very similar to a molecule called adenosine, which is naturally present in your brain. In fact, caffeine resembles adenosine so much that it can effectively block off the receptors for adenosine. This results in the feeling of alertness that you get from caffeine. The more your body relies on caffeine being in its system, the more addicted you will become.

Reason 3: Maybe it isn't addictive

Some may argue that caffeine itself isn't addictive, but anything can be addictive depending on the individual user. Some people develop addiction and dependency problems more than others. When you take into account the number of withdrawal effects - such as fatigue and headaches – for people who were drinking too much coffee and have now stopped, it's easy to see that people can indeed become addicted to coffee, regardless of whether caffeine itself is addictive.

Now then, why don't you go and make yourself a nice cup of coffee?

3 Reasons Why coffee and alcohol make us pee more

Have you noticed that you always pee more when you've been drinking coffee or alcohol? Maybe the reason for this occurrence is simply because these beverages are mostly drunk in bars and cafes, so you need a good excuse to keep leaving your awful first date or business meeting; visiting the bathroom is the perfect excuse! But do these drinks actually make us urinate more, and if so, why?

Here are three reasons why coffee and alcohol make us pee more.

Reason 1: Volume and signals

The amount of times you pee depends on the amount of fluid you drink. Whatever you are drinking, your body's natural reaction will be to eventually let it back out. Along with the volume of fluid you drink, it's the level of stimulatory signals sent to your bladder that make you urinate.

Reason 2: Caffeine

It's long been suggested that caffeine makes people pee more, which is why coffee will often have the effect. Caffeine is considered to be a diuretic. This means it actually increases the amount of urine being produced. Having said that, some doubt about this has recently been raised with some scientists claiming that caffeine has no more effect than water. It may come down to how regularly you drink caffeine too.

Reason 3: Alcohol and hormones

Alcohol is also diuretic. For every 1g of alcohol that's drunk, the urine excretion increases by about 10ml. Also, there is a hormone called Vasopressin in your body, and alcohol will reduce the production of this; meaning your kidneys will reabsorb water rather than flushing it out of the bladder. Basically, the body's natural signal shuts off allowing the bladder to fill up more with fluid, and thus making you want to pee more.

Whatever the science facts are behind this, you probably know yourself whether coffee or alcohol makes you visit the bathroom more often. If you know it does, when you're out at an important engagement, you might want to consider carefully what you have to drink. After all, you don't want to create a bad impression by disappearing to the bathroom all night.

3 Reasons Why life insurance exists

Unlike say car, or home insurance which most people would accept is a necessity. Indeed, in the case of car insurance a legal responsibility, many people still view life insurance as a nice to have instead of a "must have." Indeed, a recent survey in Great Britain was very illuminating. A research survey found that while around a quarter of Brits would be happy to insure their mobile phone, only 17% insured their life. Why do people place such little emphasis on their lives?

Here are 3 reasons why life insurance exists.

Reason 1: To ensure that bills are paid after death

One of the primary reasons of life insurance is to ensure that people don't go to their graves indebted to whomever. Although, why that would really be a problem when you are dead it is not entirely certain! Most people though like to leave their affairs in order and tie up any loose ends prior to their death and this is one way of ensuring that things like bills and funeral expenses get taken care of.

Reason 2: To ensure that loved ones are comfortable

In the same way that most people want to ensure that their funeral expenses and bills are all tied up once they have shuffled off this mortal coil, then many go to their graves a whole lot happier knowing that their kids and loved ones will be taken care of financially. There is usually enough in the life insurance pot to ensure that the mortgage on the family home gets paid and passed down to the kids. A lot of the time there is also a cash lump sum which the kids can either invest wisely, or squander at will.

Reason 3: So that the rich get richer

Although this is number three on our list, it is probably the most important reason. Because let's face it, life insurance wouldn't exist at all if the fat cats weren't getting their share of the cream. Insurance companies make a fortune on polices that become void and are aren't cashed in. Just saying!

So, while it can easily be argued that insuring your life is more important than insuring your gadgets and mobile phones be sure to shop around and make sure that you are getting the very best deal when taking out your policy.

3 Reasons Why blood sugar levels is so important

When you are young, and if you are reasonably healthy then you are probably just too busy living your life to worry too much about blood sugar levels. There is so much stuff that goes on inside our body, that we don't pay too much attention to, right? Well, yes there is, BUT even if you have no idea what your blood sugar levels are right now, you should at least take the time to understand their significance. To help you achieve that understanding, here are three reasons why blood sugar levels are so important.

Reason 1: Risk of diabetes

Diabetes comes in two forms, Type 1 and Type 2. For the purposes of this article we are only going to concern ourselves with type 2 diabetes, as that is linked directly to high blood sugar levels. Type 2 diabetes occurs when the pancreas doesn't produce enough insulin for the body to function properly. While there are some determining factors that you can't do anything about, you can at very least do something to rectify an unhealthy diet or obesity.

Reason 2 Impaired Fasting Glycaemia

This condition occurs when you are not quite at the point of diagnosis for diabetes. It is therefore, really important to have your blood sugars regularly checked. If caught at this stage, then changes to lifestyle and diet have an increased likelihood of success. Don't be put off by the fancy terminology or medical terms. Think of this simply as pre-diabetes

Reason 3: It can lead to other life-threatening conditions

Not being aware of your blood sugar levels, or having untreated diabetes can over time increase the chances of other deadly diseases such as cancer, heart attack and stroke occurring. So, it is really important that you make any lifestyle adjustments while you have the chance to do so. You don't want to regret it when it is too late.

It seems queer that having anomalies in your blood sugar, could cause such complications. However, taking regular exercise, maintaining a healthy weight and leading a balanced lifestyle can all decrease your risk and help you live a happier, healthier life.

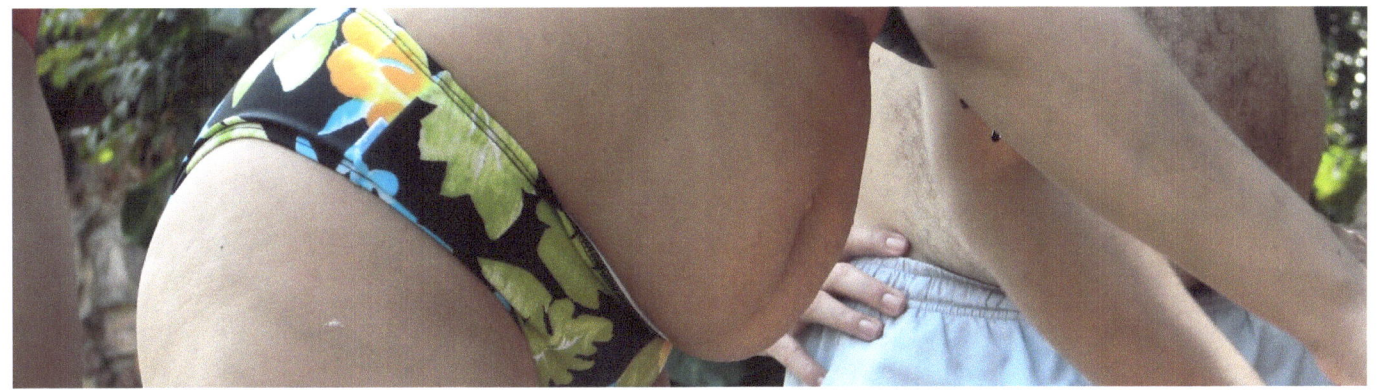

3 Reasons Why we get beer belly

Are you getting a beer belly or afraid that you might one day? Perhaps you are curious to know why people get beer bellies at all.

Here are three reasons why we get beer belly.

Reason 1: Drinking too much!

In short: people get beer bellies from drinking too much beer! If you are young and fit, it certainly won't be noticeable at first, but if you carry on drinking, there will come a day when you find that a beer belly has begun to creep up on you.

Reason 2: Too many calories

It's not beer alone that can make people's stomachs fat. Too many calories from too much food, and the wrong sort, can certainly play a part. But the beer belly itself is most recognized as being directly from drinking too much beer. When you hear that beer contains about 150 calories per unit, it is pretty obvious to see why it has such a bloating stomach effect.

Reason 3: Metabolisms slow

Beer bellies generally occur in men. At around the age of 35, most men's metabolisms begin to slow down. Whilst women will more commonly put on weight on their hips and bottoms, men tend to put weight on their bellies. The more you've been drinking and ingesting large numbers of calories, alongside a lack of exercise, the weightier you will find your stomach to be when you hit your mid-thirties.

So, if you are a male in your twenties and you are about to hit the clubs once more, you might want to consider your health a little more. It's certainly worth having fun whilst you're young, and it comes recommended, but you also don't want to completely neglect your health and wake up in ten or fifteen years' time to find that an over bloated beer belly seems to have arrived overnight! Getting the balance right is the key.

3 Reasons Why we cook food before eating

Have you ever wondered why we cook food before eating it? Here are three reasons why we cook food before eating.

Reason 1: less energy is used to digest cooked food

Although this is not always the case, the old argument states that people eat cooked food because they have to use less energy to digest it. This is certainly true of many foods, but it is not true for all.

Reason 2: Killing harmful bacteria

The main reason we cook lots of food, such as meat for example, is because it can be contaminated with harmful microbes. People do not want to become ill of course, so the food is cooked, where the high temperature of the heat will kill the microbes and make it safe to eat. Also, in some food, such as eggs, the heat causes the protein molecules to change shape.

Reason 3: People like cooked food!

Cooked food can often be a lot easier to ingest, and it can certainly improve its flavor. Everyone likes to eat fine food with a variety of tastes, textures and appearances, when they can, so that is why cooked food is so necessary: people want to enjoy food as much as they possibly can!

However, there is a good case for a raw food diet being better for the body, although this is something that is still debated in scientific circles. What is clear is that eating raw food, in some cases, helps alleviate such things as lethargy problems. So maybe you should ask yourself what's the most important thing for you when it comes to eating food. If it is for nutritional value and other health benefits, then you may want to look into the raw foods theory, as well as others. If the taste is more important, then you've got nothing to worry about. Keep cooking your food and doing what you have always done!

3 Reasons Why unhealthy foods are always so irresistible

What do you like to eat? Even if you generally eat healthily, it's likely you will have at least one guilty pleasure of eating something that's bad for you. Why do people eat unhealthy foods? Why are they always so irresistible?

Here are three reasons why unhealthy foods are always so irresistible.

Reason 1: Pleasure versus health

It's not just food. People have, perhaps, always done things that aren't necessarily good for them, whether it's more dangerous things like drugs and cigarettes or whether it's eating chocolate and fast food burgers, people will often override health being more important with pleasure being preferential!

Reason 2: What's in that tasty food?

Unhealthy foods often taste better than healthy options. That being the case, is it any wonder so many opt for pleasure over health? But why are they so tasty? It's often the case that unhealthy food tastes better because it contains lots of fat, sugar or MSG; to give just some examples. All of these things make you crave the food more than you would a stick of celery.

Reason 3: The proof's in the pudding

Deserts, puddings, chocolate bars and such things are notoriously delicious. Many people have a sweet tooth, so it's easy for such things to become irresistible. After a hard day's work and the stress of the latest household disaster, don't you deserve a nice, sugary, fattening piece of cake? Comfort food can be exactly that: comforting. It could help relieve stress. As bad as continual unhealthy eating is, it's also important to enjoy the things in life and to give yourself rewards.

So, it all comes down to getting the balance right. Many people will simply eat what they want when they want it without giving the matter any thought, but to be truly healthy and happy in equal measure, you should know what your priorities are and how you view food. Want to know more about why unhealthy food is irresistible?

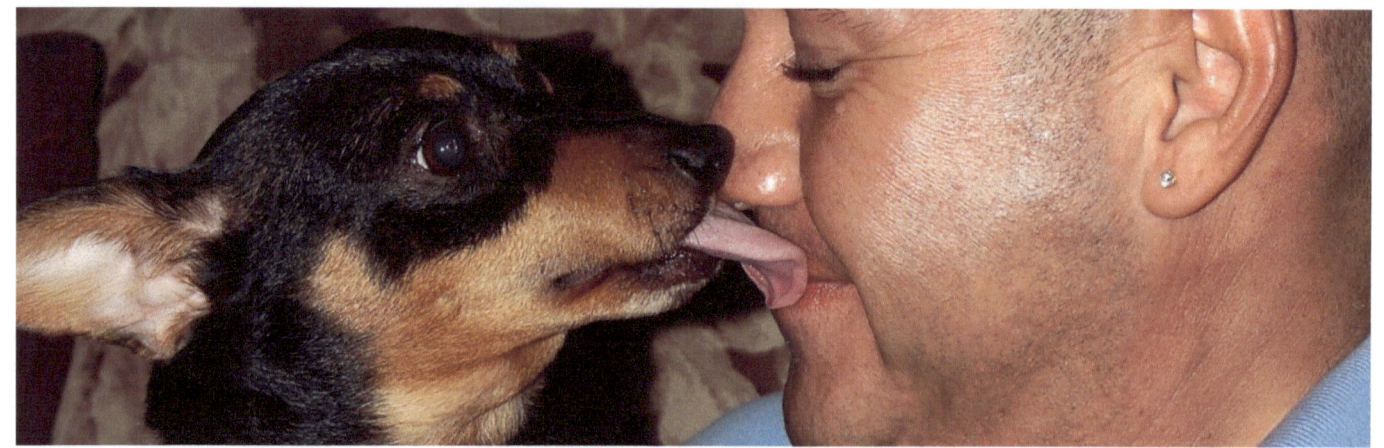

3 Reasons Why dogs lick humans affectionately

When you arrive home, your dog is at the door wagging its tail vigorously and eagerly waiting to lick your face or hand. Licking is very common among dogs especially when it comes to showing affection to its owner. It's like a normal reaction, a special kind of gesture that only dogs are born to do.

Here are three reasons why dogs lick humans affectionately.

Reason 1: It's a sign of affection

When people want to show affection, they kiss. It's actually the same with dogs. They like to lick your face and hand to show how much they love you. They enjoy doing it so much because they also like the taste of their owners. Affectionate dogs can smother your face with wet kisses especially after taking them for a walk, feeding them, or when you get home after a hard day's work or long vacation. Playing also involves some heavy licking, more so if they're given treats.

Reason 2: It releases endorphins in dogs

Licking also releases endorphins in dogs which in return give them a pleasurable and comfortable feeling. They love to lick because somehow it makes them feel happy doing so. It is also their way of relieving stress. This habit could be likened to the way people tend to bite their nails when stressed.

Reason 3: It's a habit

Did you know that mother dogs communicate with their pups by licking? Don't be surprised if your dog likes to lick because this is a habit that it has acquired from its mom. Puppies like to lick their mother's mouth as a sign of submission too. They also perform this habit to the leader of their pack. The next time your dog licks you, remember it shows that it sees you as its leader.

Licking in dogs is a natural habit. It is their way of showing affection. It gives them pleasure and comfort because it releases endorphins. They started learning to lick the moment they were born.

3 Reasons Why Many Pizzas Are Round Instead of Square or Some Other Shape

When we think of a pizza, we nearly always picture a round one. This is because almost all the big pizza chain restaurants – and many smaller, sit-down-style pizza restaurants – bake them in this shape. Read on for a few reasons why this is true.

Here are the reasons why many pizzas are round instead of square or some other shape.

Reason 1: Round Pizzas Bake More Evenly

A square or rectangular pizza has been tried by various pizza chains over the years. While they are popular with some people, the chains keep their regular round pies as their "regular" pizzas.

Part of this is the way heat circulates in a typical oven and the way it affects different shapes. In the simplest terms, a square or rectangular pizza has more edge surface than it does center, or topping, area. This means that in order to fully bake the crust, the center may burn. If, on the other hand, the pizza is baked until the center is perfectly done, the outer edges may still be undercooked. A round pizza tends to cook most evenly.

Reason 2: Round Pizzas Are What Consumers Want

Although consumers are always on the lookout for the latest, newest thing on the market, they're also extremely loyal to things they consider to be "normal." For most consumers, a round pizza seems normal, and so it's what they will naturally gravitate toward. This is why the rectangular pizzas you see advertised are usually popular for only a short while.

Reason 3: Round Pizzas Were the First Pizzas

Pizza as we know it today originated in Italy. While the Italian bakers probably didn't have a shape in mind when they baked a flatbread with toppings. Their dough was very thin, almost cracker-like in texture. This type of dough is nearly impossible to shape into a square or rectangle. Thin, stretched dough, naturally comes to rest in a rounded shape. It is usually not a perfect circle, but it will be roundish or oval in shape. This practice continued for years with nobody giving a second thought to the shape of the pizza. By the time anybody thought of it, round (or roundish) was already the accepted shape of a pizza – just like it is today!

While there is no actual rule regarding the shape of pizza, it's one of those things which are accepted as the way things have always been. Even though a few changes here and there are fun, we'll probably always go back to the round pizza.

3 Reasons Why Plates Are Round Instead of Square or Some Other Shape

If you take a look inside your kitchen, chances are good that you'll find plates – round ones. We're so used to this shape that we rarely question it. If you've ever wondered, however, why round is the standard plate shape, read on for the answers.

Here are three reasons why plates are round instead of square or some other shape.

Reason 1: Round Plates Were Easier to Make Years Ago

The first plates were made by potters. Using a potter's wheel, they created plates, bowls and other eating vessels using traditional methods. If you've ever seen a potter's wheel in action, you know that it spins in a circular motion.

Due to this spinning motion, it's only natural to assume that the first plates were round – or at least rounded at the edges – simply because that was the easiest shape to create. Creating a square, rectangular or octagonal plate on a spinning wheel would be nearly impossible. The potter would have to create a round plate, and then take it off the wheel to mold squared edges with their hands. While this would certainly have been possible, it wouldn't have been very practical.

Reason 2: We Accept Them as Standard

Since plates were made in this manner for hundreds of years, we slowly came to accept them as "normal." Even today, when we can purchase shapes in square, rectangular and virtually any shape you can imagine, we usually gravitate toward a round plate. Humans are programmed to seek out things which we feel are normal. Therefore, even though we have choices, we'll probably always prefer a round plate.

Reason 3: Food Looks Better on Round Plates

While there is a lot of disagreement over this, some people believe that the shape of our plates influences how good our food looks. You may have heard about how color influences our appetites – this is the reason why many restaurants use bright colors in their décor. Some believe that the shape of plates could have the same influence, with round plates making food look its best. The reasons for this are unclear. They could have deep psychological roots, or they could be very simple. In fact, we may think food looks better on a round plate simply because we see round plates as standard.

3 Reasons Why Beer or Soda Goes Flat When Left Open

We've all opened up a can of soda, taken a sip, set it down and then forgot about it as we got busy with something else. The result is always the same – when we come back to it, the soda is flat. The same thing happens with beer.

Here are three reasons why beer or soda goes flat when left open.

Reason 1: Carbon Dioxide Gives Soda and Beer its Fizz

When a soda is created, flavors, water and other ingredients are mixed together. Carbon dioxide is added, under high pressure and at a low temperature, to give soda its fizz and part of its taste.

The same process occurs in beer, although some of the carbon dioxide in beer is naturally occurring. Beer is brewed using a process called fermentation, in which yeast, sugars and other ingredients react with each other. This process creates several chemicals, one of which is carbon dioxide. Some brewers pour and cap beer just before the fermentation process is complete, leaving a bit of carbon dioxide – fizz – trapped inside. Other brewers add carbon dioxide to each bottle or can, ensuring that each has an adequate amount of fizz.

Reason 2: Carbon Dioxide Escapes Quickly

When you open a can of soda or beer, you hear a distinct hissing sound. This is carbon dioxide escaping. The drink will stay fizzy for a while, with visible bubbles. Over time, however, all the bubbles will rise to the surface and pop, allowing the carbon dioxide to escape. By the time this process is over, the drink is called "flat," having no fizz left. It doesn't taste as good, and most people will pour it out and open a fresh can or bottle.

Reason 3: Bubbles in Sparkling Wine

Another example of a fizzy beverage is sparkling wine. Champagne is probably the most recognizable sparkling wine, but many other delicious varieties exist. There are two ways by which bubbles get into sparkling wine. One is very quick, and is essentially the same way bubbles get into soda – wine is bottled, and then injected with carbon dioxide. The other, slightly more expensive and time consuming way is to allow the wine to ferment almost all the way, then bottle and cap it – this is the same method many beer brewers use.

3 Reasons Why Hair Turns Gray as We Grow Old

Whether we like it or not, we grow old eventually. One of the signs you're not getting any younger is that your hair changes color. As we age, our hair turns either white or gray. While this happens to some people later in life than others, it will happen to everybody sooner or later.

Here are the reasons why hair turns gray as we grow old.

Reason 1: Color is Caused by Melanin

All the color in our skin and hair is caused by a substance called melanin. The amount of melanin in our bodies determines whether we have light or dark hair and skin. In our scalps, each hair grows out of what is called a follicle. Inside each hair follicle is a tiny cell called a melanocyte. This gives hair its color. Our hair color – along with skin and eye color – is determined by our genetics.

As we get older, our bodies naturally produce less melanin. This is why the eyes of some very old people seem to fade in color, and it's also why they have gray, silver or white hair. Melanin production slows down gradually. In some people, this doesn't begin until they are in their 50s, while a small percentage of people see their first gray hair as early as high school.

Reason 2: Fright Can Trigger White Hair

You may have heard people say that somebody was frightened so much that their hair turned white. While we usually say this in a joking manner, it can really happen – just not as abruptly as the legends say.

The reason behind aging white hair is, simply put, that parts of our bodies get tired as we get older. An extremely bad scare can literally age the body so sharply that the melanocytes cease production. This doesn't mean that existing hair turns white – only bleach could do that – but it can mean that, immediately after the fright, new hair growth will be white or gray.

Reason 3: Chronic Stress Can Mean Early Grays

You may have heard people say that a certain situation is "giving them gray hair." While, like hair turning white, this is an exaggeration, it does have roots in fact. Chronic stress is likely to contribute to early grays. People with stressful childhoods are more likely to go gray earlier in life if that stress is not properly addressed. Likewise, people with extremely stressful jobs often go gray far earlier than their peers with more relaxed professions.

As you can see, even the simplest changes to the human body often have complex causes. It could be caused by lack of melanin, feeling frightful most of the time, or being under chronic stress.

BEAUTY

3 Reasons Why we blush

Have you ever wondered why humans blush? Maybe you're somebody who blushes a lot and you've just turned red at the mention of it! Well, if you're curious to know the answer, here are 3 reasons as to why we blush.

Reason 1: Emotional triggers

Commonly, blushing occurs because of embarrassment. Perhaps your toddler has shouted out a rude word in the middle of a busy supermarket. Maybe your blind date has walked out of the restaurant after tipping a glass of wine over your head. Are you nervous about a presentation that you need to make? Whatever the occurrence might be, if something's made you feel embarrassed, it's very probable that you have turned red! Blushing is one of those human-only physiological traits that sets us apart from the rest of the animal kingdom. After all, you won't see a pigeon blushing!

Reason 2: The physiology

So, embarrassment - along with shyness, shame or stress – can turn the color of your skin a certain shade of vermillion, but why does this happen in the first place? What are the physiological circumstances for such a peculiar occurrence? Well, the reddening of the face comes about as a result of the emotional trigger (being embarrassed, for instance) stimulating your nervous system, which causes the blood vessels in your face to widen. It's the increase of the flow of blood into the blood vessels underneath the skin which turns your face red.

Reason 3: Other factors

As well as emotional responses causing blushing, there are some other factors that can also make face reddening occur. These include: alcohol consumption, eating spicy food, sudden hot or cold temperatures, strenuous exercise and specific medical problems.

It's true that some people will blush more than others, but at the same time, everyone has experienced what it's like to go red in the face with embarrassment. So there's no need to feel ashamed at blushing; after all, that will only make you blush more!

3 Reasons Why men have nipples

Have you ever wondered why men have nipples? After all, the reason for female nipples existing is for the production of milk. This is an obvious and well-known fact, but male nipples, on the other hand, provide no such function. So why do men have nipples at all? If you are interested to know the answers, here are 3 solid reasons.

Reason 1: Believe it or not, all embryos actually start off as female in their blueprint!

Every embryo starts off life with a female blueprint – and this blueprint includes nipples! After about 60 days, for those Y chromosomes that are destined to be male, the hormone testosterone begins to set in. So, that is why we biologically have nipples.

Reason 2: Did nipples of the prehistoric man have a function?

Perhaps the question should then be: why do male nipples have nerves and blood vessels? Did they perhaps serve a function in the prehistoric past? There is a lack of evidence for the idea that prehistoric men once fed their babies in the way that women now do, but it remains a hypothesis nevertheless. Whatever the nipples' original function may have, or not, been, it is likely that any function they did have was removed over time by natural selection.

Reason 3: Male nipples are erogenous zones

Many people will say that male nipples exist because they are erogenous zones which aid sexual satisfaction. So surely that should be a good enough reason as to why men have nipples, shouldn't it?

There are various different viewpoints about the subject to be had, so if you are curious to know more, be sure to do your own research and come to your own conclusions!

3 Reasons Why men have chin beards

Why do men have beards? Have you ever stopped to ask that question? Well, whether you have or not, now the question has been posed, you will surely want some answers!

Here are 3 reasons why men have chin beards.

Reason 1: Hormones

Men can grow beards whilst women can't, due to hormones. Men have more androgens than women, which is ultimately what causes the hair growth on men's faces.

Reason 2: Fashions of the times

But why do men grow their hair? Many will shave because they prefer the smooth look, whilst others not only grow their beards but proudly adorn them! Why is this? It could simply be put down to personal taste, but often it will have to do with the fashion of a particular era. Look back at different times in recent and ancient history and you will see that different peoples in different times would tend to adopt beards more than others.

Reason 3: Masculinity

In the present day, chin beards have become more fashionable once again. As well as any social trends that may be occurring, it's probable that a lot of men grow their beards to feel manly. There's something about the growth of facial hair, which sets men apart from women, which is an ultimate symbol of masculinity; presumably backdating to ancient times when cavemen would have just grown their hair; personal grooming not being too high up their agendas at that time.

There are many theories as to why men have chin beards. It's often the case that the so-called goatee beard is associated with hipsters/artists/musicians, and a recent study has looked into why this might be. There are other theories and studies as well, so if you want to learn more about beards, be sure to do some research of your own.

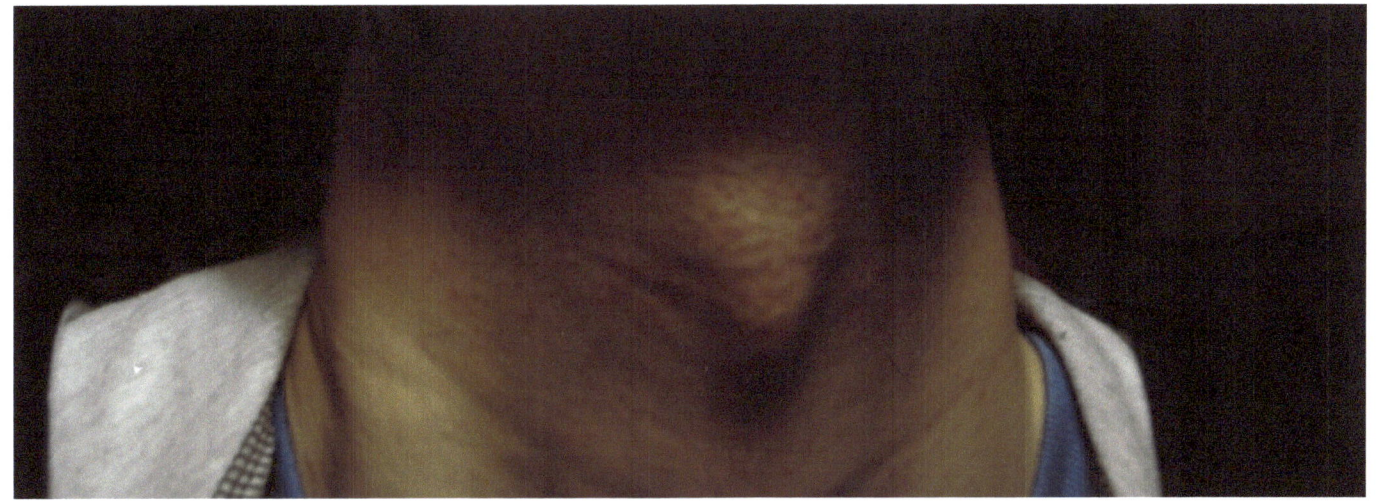

3 Reasons Why women don't have Adam's Apples as men do

Adam's apples are very prominent among men, but why can't you see the Adam's Apple on a woman? The Adam's apple is another term for larynx, or the voice box, and the larynx gives us our voice. This allows us to make different sounds, from laughing, to shouting or singing. It's called Adam's Apple based on the story of how Adam ate the forbidden fruit that got stuck in his throat.

Here are the reasons why women don't have Adam's apples as men do.

Reason 1: Enlargement of a boy's larynx
Boys and girls experience different changes in their body once they enter puberty. Girls start to menstruate while boys grow teste drop. One of the most noticeable changes in boys is that their larynx grows bigger. This enlargement of the larynx on men is referred to the Adam's Apple. Girls' larynx grows too but it's very seldom that we see it protruding the way we do with boys'.

Reason 2: Bigger voice, bigger voice box.
One obvious reason why men have Adam's apple is because they have bigger, deeper, and louder voices. Can you imagine what their voice may sound like if their larynx is similar to that of women? It would be hilarious to hear such a small voice coming from a manly body. A women's voice is softer and smaller because their larynx isn't that big.

Reason 3: A built-in lie detector
Perhaps men were created to have bigger Adam's apples because they serve as an excellent lie detector. In fact, many men are embarrassed at having one, especially if it's so big that they bob when you're swallowing food. In addition, people can tell if you're nervous because the Adam's apple has the tendency to jump uncontrollably if you're feeling just that like when you're lying or performing in front of an audience.

Women don't have Adam's Apples like men do because they have smaller voice boxes. Men have bigger and deeper voices that require a big larynx. Many men are embarrassed about their large Adam's Apple because it gives away their emotions easily.

HEALTH

3 Reasons Why eating healthy is important but hard to do in America

People are aware of the importance of eating healthy, especially in staying fit and away from sickness. However, there are still those who find it hard to do, especially in America. Poor diet is considered a major cause of all kinds of diseases like heart attack, stroke, and diabetes, but despite the efforts of the government and private organizations, many Americans still encounter difficulty when it comes to eating the right food. In fact, the National Alliance for Nutrition and Activity revealed that poor diet contributes to one of the leading causes of death in the U.S.

Here are the reasons why eating healthy is important but hard to do in America.

Reason 1: Hectic schedules prevent Americans from cooking their own food

Many experts believe that eating healthy comes from cooking your own food. However, not all Americans have the luxury of time. They are always on the run, keeping not just one but two to three jobs in order to make both ends meet. They have to wake up in the morning with no time to exercise or cook breakfast but only grab a cup of coffee and a doughnut from a nearby café. In the evening, dinner tends to be a burger and fries from a fast food chain.

Reason 2: Lack of health education

Based on a survey conducted by the Physicians Committee for Responsible Medicine in 2012, a lack of education on calories, cholesterol, fats and the like is one of the factors to blame for America's unhealthy eating habits. Add to that the fact that many children follow in the footsteps of their parents. If they see their parents skipping meals or eating junk foods, they too will follow such habits.

Reason 3: Convenience

Did you know that Americans consume more packaged food than fresh ones? That's because packaged foods are their more practical choice especially if they're too busy to cook their meals. For example, they can easily buy ready to eat foods in cans as well as microwaveable ones.

Eating healthy is important, but many Americans still find it hard to do. It could be because they don't have time to prepare their own food or were not properly educated on healthy eating habits. Finally, many Americans no longer eat fresh foods but instead buy processed ones to satisfy their hunger.

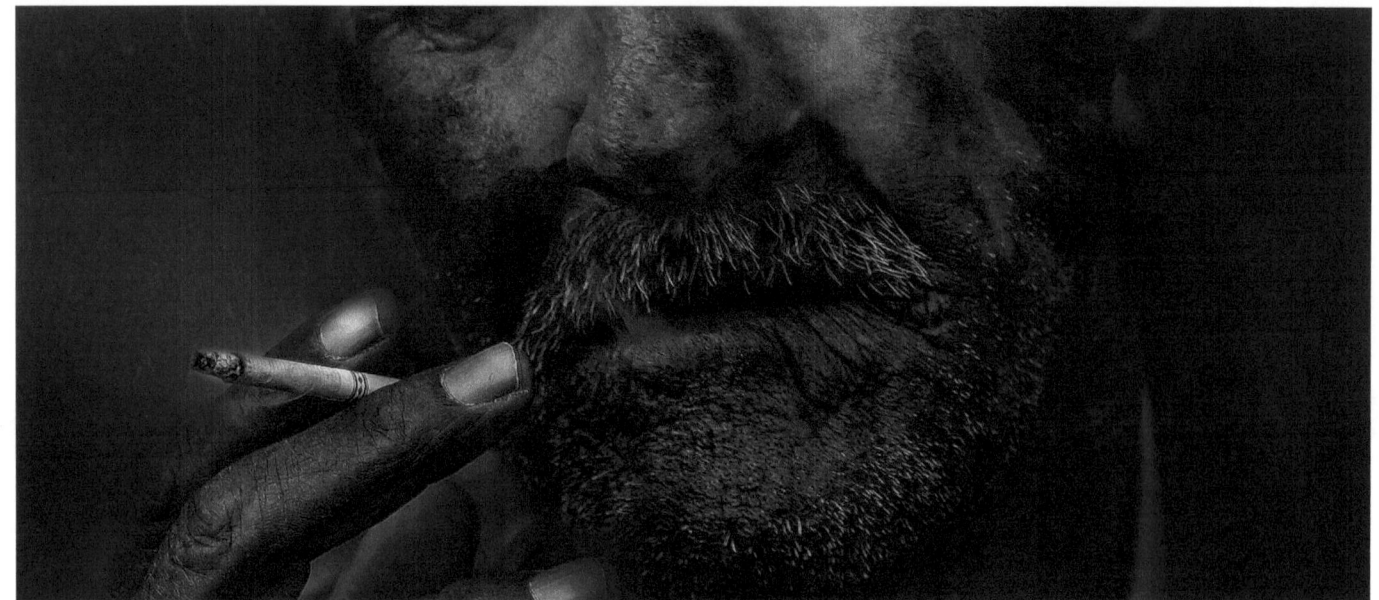

3 Reasons Why smoking is absolutely bad for your health and wallet

Smoking is dangerous to your health. Yes, we hear and see this slogan all the time. It can be found in cigarette packs and advertised on television. Health agencies even came up with posters that show the ill effects of smoking as a warning to those who smoke or intend to do so. But what are the real reasons for this anti-smoking movement?

Here are the reasons why smoking is absolutely bad for your health and wallet.

Reason 1: It damages the respiratory system

The most common effect of smoking on one's health is the fact that it damages the respiratory system. This is because every time you inhale smoke, you take in substances that are damaging to your organs, especially the lungs. Regular smoking will cause your lungs to lose their ability to filter these harmful chemicals, and coughing alone won't be enough. This is why many smokers have lung cancer, emphysema, and are more prone to respiratory infections.

Reason 2: It damages the heart

The heart is one of the major and most important organs of the body because it is responsible for circulating blood. Smoking can damage the heart because of the presence of carbon monoxide and nicotine. These chemicals can increase the risk of smokers to have heart attacks and heart-related diseases like cerebrovascular and peripheral vascular diseases. According to the NHS, smoking in fact doubles your risk of heart attack and the risk of dying due to heart disease compared to those who don't smoke.

Reason 3: It's an expensive habit

Aside from being bad for your health, smoking is also bad to your wallet. That's because cigarettes aren't free—you have to pay for them. According to The AWL, New York has the most expensive cigarette price which amounts to $14.50 per pack. If you're a regular smoker, you will be consuming at least a pack per day and multiply that with the number of days a month and you could be spending an average of $435 on cigarettes a month. That's a large amount of money you could have used to pay for rent or food.

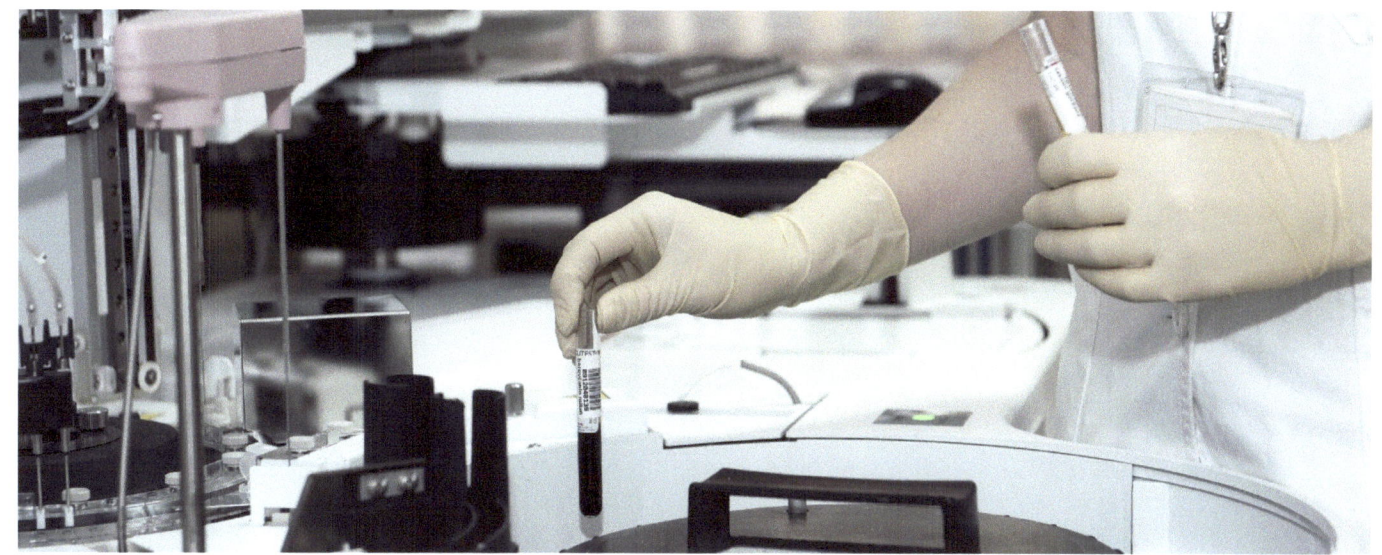

3 Reasons Why Medicare is not sustainable

Medicare is a federal insurance program in the United States of America that offers medical insurance to certain groups of people, most notably the over sixty-fives, younger people with specific medical conditions, as well as people suffering from kidney failure that is not expected to get any better. Depending upon which side of the fence you happen to be sitting on there are numerous arguments both for and against it.

Here are just 3 of the reasons why people would argue that Medicare is not sustainable:

Reason 1: Increased taxation

To his credit, Obama had a noble vision when introducing Obamacare. It is after all perfectly reasonable to suggest that people from the poorest demographics in society should be entitled to medical protection and have access to life-saving treatments and drugs. Unfortunately, this comes with a price tag, most notably in the form of increased taxation. Taxes that hit the wealthy, may be popular with the poorest in society. However, when it is the wealthy that has funds to lobby against these taxes, it is easy to see how Obamacare could be shot down.

Reason 2: The process of filing tax returns becomes more complicated

It is generally accepted that the IRS doesn't exactly make it easy for citizens to file their returns. Obamacare, rather than simplifying matters actually makes things more difficult. It also hits millions of poor Americans, who don't quite qualify for the Federal Poverty Level Limit. People who do qualify have to then fill out 8962 premium tax form.

Reason 3: There are narrow windows for enrollment

Rather than being able to enroll all year round, which would seem logical, citizens can only get cover during specific annual open enrollment periods. This places strain on the system, and leaves people who don't manage to enroll on time without cover.

3 Reasons Why the Paleo Diet is buzzing in healthy eating circles

Can you imagine eating the same stuff as your ancestors 10,000 years ago? That's exactly what the Paleo diet is all about. It is commonly referred to as the caveman diet because the foods you eat on this diet are similar to those which people used to eat during the Paleolithic era. Think about no fast food, no fancy restaurants, and no microwave.

Here are three reasons why the Paleo diet is buzzing in healthy eating circles.

Reason 1: Load up on fruits and vegetables

One of the secrets behind the success of the Paleo diet is the fact that it consists mostly of fruits and vegetables. The Paleo diet is a clean diet because you aren't eating processed foods with preservatives or additives. Since fruits and vegetables are rich in nutrients and fiber, you won't feel as hungry. This diet also eliminates bloating and leaves you with a flatter stomach.

Reason 2: Weight loss benefits

Many dieters are looking for the right diet that will help them lose weight effectively, and the Paleo diet is the answer. As far as losing weight is concerned, studies prove that it is very effective. For instance, a study comparing the effects of the Paleo diet to the effects of those with the low-fat diet involving 70 obese postmenopausal women proved that those who were under the Paleo diet lost 14.3 pounds. On the other hand, those on a low-fat diet lost only 5.7 pounds.

Reason 3: Healthier brain

The Paleo diet isn't only good for the body—it's beneficial to the brain, too. This diet suggests eating food sources rich in protein and fat including cold water fish like salmon. These fish are rich in omega 3 fatty acids which the average American diet lacks. They have DHA, which is beneficial to one's eyes, heart, and brain development. Other sources of omega 3 fatty acids are pasture-raised meats and eggs.

The Paleo diet is buzzing in healthy eating circles because it is the ideal diet for people who want to lose weight. Under this diet, one eats lots of fruits and vegetables as well as meat rich in protein and omega 3 fatty acids. It has been tested and proven an effective and safe weight loss diet which is healthy for the brain as well.

3 Reasons Why eating spoiled food which has been cooked still make us sick

Wouldn't it be wonderful if foods didn't have expirations dates? Just imagine how much you would be able to save on groceries every month! Eating spoiled food can cause serious health problems such as food poisoning. Even if you have already cooked your food, once it goes beyond its point of being safe and edible, eating it can be poisonous. Spoiled food is no different from foods which have already expired.

Reason 1: They contain harmful bacteria

According to WebMD, the Salmonella enterica bacterium can cause food poisoning known as salmonellosis. It is commonly found in beef, poultry and eggs. Sometimes, this bacterium can be transmitted by animals like turtles, hamsters, and rodents. Eating spoiled food even if it was cooked is a big no especially if it contains such ingredients like beef. Chances are, salmonella has already infected it even if you will reheat or recook the whole thing.

Reason 2: They're contaminated

Aside from the famous salmonella, spoiled food can also be contaminated with other bacteria such as listeria. Just like salmonella, eating foods contaminated by listeria can cause food poisoning known as listeriosis. Sometimes, the produce we use in preparing our food as well as processed food items like cheeses are prone to being contaminated with listeria. If the food itself is already spoiled, it goes to show that there are many contaminants present in it. Eating it will only cause you your health.

Reason 3: They are unhealthy

Food components start to disintegrate the moment they begin to spoil. They actually undergo several physical and chemical changes that they eventually lose their taste and nutrients. Can you imagine eating a bad-smelling steak or a moldy piece of bread? Although they have undergone the process of cooking, they are already unhealthy.

Eating spoiled food which you have cooked can cause food poisoning, vomiting, dizziness, intestinal cramps, diarrhea and other discomforts. They will make you sick because they have bacteria and other contaminants. They are also unhealthy.

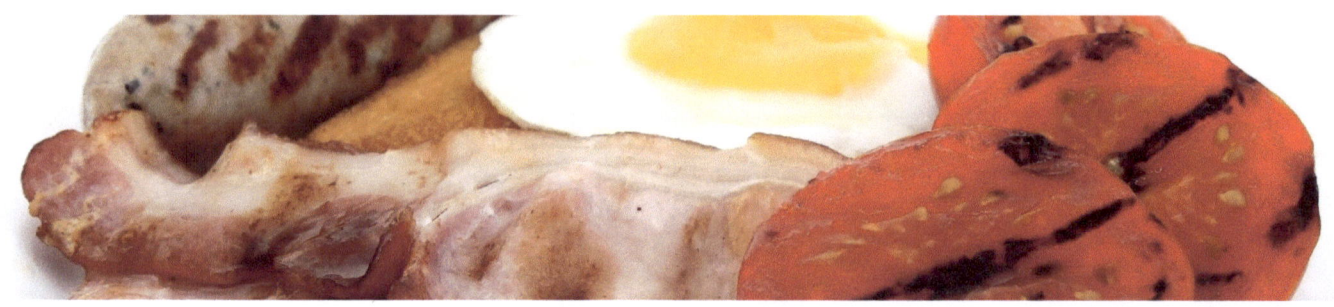

3 Reasons Why cholesterol is bad

Heart diseases, cardiac arrest and strokes are very common nowadays. That's because people don't care much about their health especially if they're still young. They eat whatever they want and have sedentary lifestyles. They are also exposed to many stressors at work, at home, and even in their environment. Once they experience heart problems, they blame cholesterol. Based on what people have heard and learned from health experts, cholesterol is bad. Actually, it is the LDL or low-density lipoprotein which is considered as a bad type of cholesterol.

Here are the reasons why cholesterol is bad.

Reason 1: It causes stroke

Bad cholesterol or LDL is one of the major causes of stroke. Once there's too much of this cholesterol in your body, it forms into thick plaques that block arteries from transporting blood into the brain. When this happens, the brain doesn't get sufficient supply of oxygen and will damage brain cells and cause them to die. Stroke has symptoms including a feeling of numbness and weakness as well as difficulty in speaking or moving.

Reason 2: It causes heart attack

LDL buildups in the arteries make it difficult for blood to flow through the heart. In case a part of this plaque breaks, blood clot will occur and it won't be long before you have a heart attack. Once there's insufficient supply of blood to the heart, the victim will experience chest discomfort and pain. Some even feel pain in their shoulders, neck, back, and jaw. The heart is literally dying and if blood follow is not restored immediately, it can lead to death.

Reason 3: It causes gallstones

High cholesterol causes bile imbalance and eventually cause gallstones to form in the kidneys. As a matter of fact, cholesterol stones comprise 80 percent of these gallstones. Further, plaque buildup prevents proper blood flow to the kidneys and even the stomach. Some of the common symptoms are pain in the abdominal area, vomiting, and nausea.

LDL or bad cholesterol can damage one's overall health and wellness. It can cause all kinds of diseases such as stroke, heart attack, and gallstones.

3 Reasons Why cholesterol is good

When it comes to heart-related diseases, many are convinced that cholesterol is to blame. But contrary to what others believe, cholesterol is not all bad. The HDL or high-density lipoprotein is considered the good cholesterol. It is denser than its counterpart, LDL or low-density lipoprotein. Unlike with the bad cholesterol, HDL ensures stability of our body cells.

Here are the reasons why cholesterol is good.

Reason 1: Reduces risk of heart disease

Did you know that HDL cholesterol is good for you because they serve as scavengers of the body? They help remover LDL or bad cholesterol that tends to buildup in the walls of the arteries. LDL is the suspect behind many heart diseases and with high amounts of HDL, you can be protected. Good cholesterol recycles its bad counterpart by taking it to the liver where it will be reprocessed.

Reason 2: HDL keeps blood vessels healthy

Blood vessels are responsible in transporting blood throughout the body. When there's a lot of plaque buildups due to LDL, these vessels become clogged and cause heart attack or stroke. Thanks to HDL, blood vessels can facilitate the proper flow of blood to all parts of the body especially the brain. It works by scrubbing the endothelium or the inner walls of the blood vessels to keep them in excellent working condition.

Reason 3: Reduces LDL

It is safe to say that HDL acts like knights in shining armor of the body with the LDL as the villains. We are all aware that LDL can lead to serious health complications and even death. Aside from switching to a healthier habit and regular exercise, one also needs to reduce the amount of LDL in the bloodstream. This is why doctors recommend taking food high in HDL. As knights, they stop LDL from building plaques and eliminate them from the body.

Good cholesterol is essential to the body. It can lower the risk of heart disease, keeps blood vessels healthy, and reduces LDL level.

3 Reasons Why health gurus recommend having a healthy breakfast

Breakfast is the most important meal of the day and for good reason. It's called as such because it breaks the fast that the body undergoes when it's asleep at night. When you wake up, you need to recharge after spending numerous hours not consuming anything. This is why eating breakfast is a must.

Here are the reasons why health gurus recommend having a healthy breakfast.

Reason 1: It fuels the body

Breakfast fuels the body to function properly throughout the day. It keeps you physically active while doing different activities. Nutritionists advise that one should eat breakfast within two hours upon waking up. In addition, a healthy breakfast should provide you with calories of up to 20% to 35% of your GDA or guideline daily allowance. Your breakfast should consist of foods which are rich in calcium, iron, protein, fiber, and B vitamins to ensure you stay at your best throughout the day.

Reason 2: It helps the brain to function well

Health gurus recommend eating breakfast because it benefits the brain. As a matter of fact, they highly recommend children and adults to eat their breakfast before going to school or work. The American Dietetic Association as mentioned by WebMD claimed that children who eat their breakfast are likely to perform better in class than those who don't. They are more attentive and have better eye-hand coordination.

Reason 3: It prevents overeating

Eating breakfast improves the metabolism and reduces your chances of consuming foods with high calories. In a way, it helps prevent overeating which is oftentimes the result of skipping meals. If you're on a diet, it's a must to eat breakfast because once starvation kicks in, you'll want to eat something sweet or fatty or anything that'll provide you the energy you'll need.

Health gurus recommend having a healthy breakfast because it provides the body the energy it needs. It also helps the brain to function well so you perform better at work or in school. Moreover, it improves metabolism so you avoid overeating.

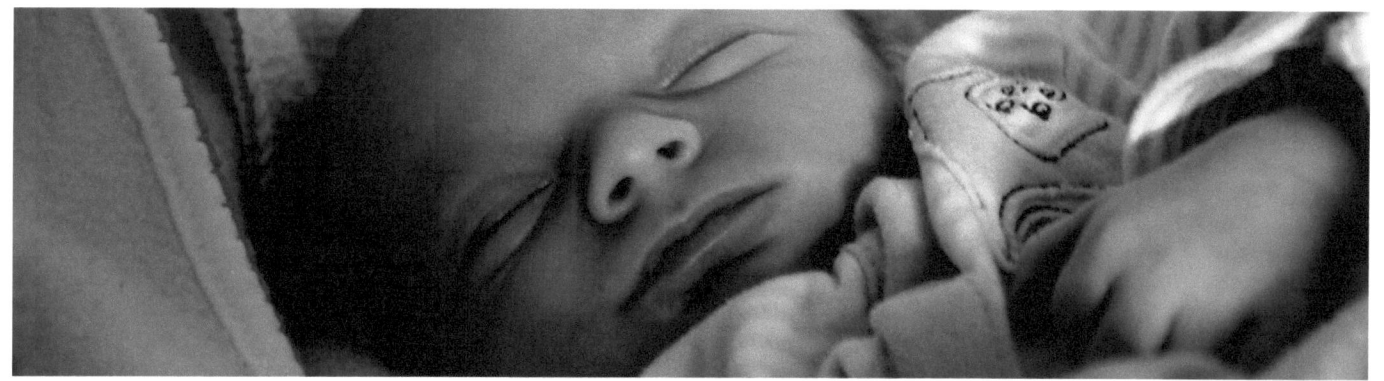

3 Reasons Why we sleep

Have you ever stopped to ask yourself: why do we sleep? It's such an everyday (or every-night) part of life, that it's easy to take it for granted. When you're tired, you sleep. Simple. But why do we need to sleep?

Here are three reasons why we sleep.

Reason 1: Recharging

Sleeping is our way of re-energizing. We eat food to give us energy and we sleep to recharge. Just like a cellphone running low on battery, your body needs to rest in order to work properly. It seems obvious that our body usage in the day creates tiredness which produces sleep.

Reason 2: Cognitive skills

Having stated the above common sense point of view, when you begin to look at things in more detail, you'll realize that scientists still aren't exactly sure why we sleep. The belief that the body needs to recuperate could actually be wrong. After all, in reality, the amount of energy saved by sleeping is only 50 kCal- a miniscule amount! More important than recharging then, it is these factors that are most relevant: without sleep, it would be difficult to maintain everyday cognitive skills like speaking, memory use and flexible thinking. So sleeping has more of an effect on recharging the brain than it does the rest of the body.

Reason 3: Feeling better

Whatever the scientific reasons for sleeping are, everyone knows that they feel better after a good night's sleep. Not only are things like cognitive skills affected, it's also plain that if you haven't had enough sleep, it's likely you will be in a terribly grumpy mood! In fact, you only have to look at the effects extreme insomnia has on some people to see how much a good sleep is required. A lack of sleep can lead to all sorts of things like depression and even hallucinations!

3 Reasons Why we need to drink water to stay alive

Do you drink enough water? It's recommended that you should drink around 2 liters a day, and it's generally assumed that if you go without any water for more than 5 days, you could be in danger of dying. So why do we need to drink water to stay alive?

Here are three reasons why we need to drink water to stay alive.

Reason 1: The body needs to function

Two-thirds of your body is water. The vast majority of you and the Earth is water. Yet, it is still constantly required to maintain health, well-being, and ultimately life itself. Human beings require water for: circulation, respiration and conversion of food into energy.

Reason 2: The body loses water

Despite us containing so much water and replenishing it all the time, we still lose a huge amount of water constantly as well; through things like sweating and urinating. You even lose water through the act of breathing.

Reason 3: Dehydration

When you don't drink enough water, dehydration will occur. This can cause things like headaches, tiredness and losing concentration. Long-term dehydration can be more dangerous, leading to things like damage of the kidneys.

So, human beings need water to survive and each day you need to replace 2.4 liters (about 2.5 quarts) of water through foods or liquids. The best sources of food that contain water are fruit and vegetables; which obviously also contain plenty of other vitamins that will be good for your body. The best source of water in fluid form is, not surprisingly, a glass of good old H_2O water itself. So remember to look after yourself and drink plenty of water. It's easy to forget to do such things amongst the fast pace of the world, but just think how fortunate you are that you're able to replenish your water by simply turning on a tap. There are plenty of people in the world that have either no access to clean water or no water at all. In fact, staggeringly, 783 million people in the world don't have access to clean water.

3 Reasons Why binge drinking is terrible for you

Researchers refer to binge drinking as consuming eight or more units of alcohol for men and six or more units for women in only one session. But then this definition isn't applicable to everybody because it still depends on the tolerance level of the person drinking and how fast that session is.

Here are the reasons why binge drinking is terrible for you.

Reason 1: It causes drunkenness and a hangover

Alcoholic drinks can cause drunkenness. It's that feeling when one's mind becomes foggy and lightheaded. You are dizzy and your speech becomes slurry. You also want to vomit. The next day you'll experience a hangover, which makes your head throb like somebody's drilling into your skull. You're most likely to be dehydrated, too, after losing fluids from vomiting and urinating. There are instances when you actually black out and forget what happened the night before.

Reason 2: It causes alcohol poisoning

Severe case of binge drinking can lead to death because of alcohol poisoning. That's because an alcohol overdose can cause you to stop breathing and even stop your heart from functioning. If you're vomiting, you could choke and block the passage of air. Alcohol poisoning can also cause seizures, shortness of breath, low body temperature, and paleness, among other symptoms.

Reason 3: It impairs judgment

Binge drinking is hazardous not only to one's health but to one's mind as well. Its most common effect is that it impairs judgment. This means when you've been binge drinking you're likely to do something risky which you won't do at all when you're in the right state of mind. You can injure yourself and others, too, because walking or driving becomes difficult for you.

Binge drinking is not a healthy habit. It causes drunkenness and hangover and impairs judgment, too. It can also be deadly because it can cause alcohol poisoning. In some cases, binge drinking can lead to death due to health issues or driving under the influence.

3 Reasons Why we get diabetes

There are two types of diabetes. People either have Type 1 or Type 2 conditions, with about 90% of people having Type 2. The latter develops as a result of the body not being able to make enough insulin (a hormone made in the pancreas), whereas in Type 1, the body isn't able to effectively use insulin. There is no common factor to fit every type of diabetes and individual with the condition, but why do we get diabetes at all?

Here are 3 reasons why we get diabetes.

Reason 1: Type 1 diabetes

So, although there is no specific cause of Type 1 diabetes, the following things may certainly be contributory factors: a viral or bacterial infection, toxins in food, an unidentified component causing autoimmune reaction, or a genetic disposition.

Reason 2: Type 2 diabetes

In Type 2 diabetes, there are usually various factors involved, but often it's the case that there's a family history of Type 2 diabetes. Other causes for Type 2 include: obesity, increasing age, a bad diet, pregnancy and a sedentary lifestyle.

Reason 3: Gestational diabetes

Diabetes in pregnancy is known as gestational diabetes and little is known about its causes. Having said that, there are a number of factors that could increase the risk of developing the condition. These include: suffering from polycystic ovary syndrome, giving birth to a baby over 9 lbs, obesity, and a family history of gestational diabetes. It can also be related to ethnicity as some groups are more prone to developing this type of diabetes.

3 Reasons Why Vitamin C is important in the diet

Whether it's through food or through supplements, it is vital that you take vitamins for maintaining good health and wellbeing. Vitamin C in particular is an important one to have in your diet, but why is this?

Here are 3 reasons why vitamin C is important in the diet.

Reason 1: It keeps your cells healthy

Vitamin C is also known as ascorbic acid and it has many benefits. It keeps your cells healthy, it helps wounds to heal and vitamin C is necessary for the maintenance of healthy connective tissue.

Reason 2: You don't want to get scurvy!

If you don't have enough vitamin C in your diet, it can lead to things like scurvy. Vitamin C is needed to make collagen – which is a type of protein that's contained in different tissues like skin, bones and cartilage. When collagen isn't sufficiently produced it can create scurvy. Symptoms of this include pain in muscles and joints, tiredness, the bleeding and swelling of gums, and red spots appearing on the skin.

Reason 3: Vitamin C isn't produced by your body

Some vitamins can be created by the body, but this isn't the case for vitamin C. That's why it's so important that you have it regularly in your diet. As long as you eat the right things, you won't get any nasty things like scurvy. Eat plenty of fruit and vegetables and maintain a balanced diet to make sure you stay healthy.

It's recommended that you should have five portions of fruit and veg a day (which can include things like smoothies). As long as you keep to this simple recommendation, and maintain a balanced diet alongside being cautious with the consumption of alcohol and other stimulants, you should find that you're as fit as a fiddle!

3 Reasons Why we have pain

There are very few things in this world that are worse from a gnawing toothache, or the pain that you feel when breaking your leg. Aside from the physiological pain that people feel when they get injured, there is also the emotional pain of having one's heart broken. Pain is a difficult concept to define, and what hurts one person, may be nothing more than a minor irritation to someone else.

Here are three reasons why we have pain.

Reason 1: Illness

All right, so this might not be a revolutionary concept. However, illness is the biggest cause of pain within all living creatures. In the same way that physical illness can cause physical pain, then mental illnesses such as schizophrenia and depression can cause emotional pain that is incredibly difficult for non-sufferers to understand. Drugs are given to alleviate the pain. However, it is only by getting to the root cause of the problem that the pain can be truly eased.

Reason 2: It's a defense mechanism

Most people probably haven't thought about it in these terms. However, in the most basic sense it is a defense mechanism; an early warning system that tells us that we have been injured and that we need to stop and investigate. So, okay if you have just grazed your knee then the pain will generally go away very quickly, whereas the more badly injured you are, the more the pain will increase and intensify. Interestingly enough, studies have shown that pain can actually be a good thing. Pain keeps us alive with those with higher pain thresholds frequently outliving those with lower ones.

Reason 3: Phantom pain

An article on pain wouldn't be complete without at least briefly mentioning phantom pain. This usually occurs when someone has had a limb amputated and is the body's way of dealing with the loss and processing it.

While very few people would wish pain on anyone, no matter how much they have wronged them, it is interesting to think that every time you jam your finger accidentally in the door, your body is simply trying to alert you by causing you tremendous amounts of pain. Who would have thought that as humans we could be so masochistic?

3 Reasons Why we get heart diseases and heart attacks

Heart Disease and Cancer are still the biggest killers in the Western world, and if you were to take a straw poll of random people and ask them what diseases they feared most, would be right up there. Trying to re-educate the public and change their lifestyles has become the number one priority of most governments, who facing an ever ageing population and the need to impose austerity measures are looking to cut back on their healthcare provision. So, in case you have been living on a completely different planet, here are 3 reasons why we get heart disease and heart attacks.

Reason 1: Our arteries become blocked

Okay, so at first glance that may appear as if heart disease is an unavoidable condition that just happens to people. Wrong. Blocked arteries occur primarily as a result of an unhealthy lifestyle. When someone has a heart attack, symptoms can include any of the following, searing pain in the chest, dizziness, the patient may be sweaty or clammy. Unfortunately, many people don't even realize that their arteries are blocked until they actually suffer a heart attack. However, the good news is that it is never too late to change your lifestyle.

Reason 2: Poor lifestyle

If you have a bad diet, don't exercise, drink too much caffeine, are constantly stressed and don't get enough sleep then you are a prime candidate for heart disease and heart attacks. However, ANY positive change to your lifestyle can make a difference. Just because you have reached your forties, doesn't mean to say that you can't begin to do things differently. If anything, that is a perfect reason to make changes. You don't have to make all of the changes overnight.

Reason 3: Hereditary conditions

Contrary to the information out there, lifestyle is NOT the only cause of heart disease. Some people are born with heart defects, and while some heart defects are treatable or heal completely in childhood, many heart defects never heal. People born with heart defects are even more susceptible to heart attacks and heart disease as they get older.

No-one can predict the future. However, it is widely accepted that by making some basic and simple lifestyle changes everyone can significantly reduce their chances of heart disease and ultimately suffering from a heart attack.

3 Reasons Why we get strokes

Strokes are generally one of those medical occurrences that terrifies people and because they can kill in an instant are up there alongside heart attacks and cancer. A stroke in the simplest of terms is an attack of the brain that occurs when all or part of the blood supply to the brain is cut off. Strokes are deadly and can come on without warning. The most obvious signs that someone is having a stroke is slurred speech, weakness in the left side, and a drooping of one side of the mouth. If you suspect that someone is having a stroke, then you should seek emergency medical help immediately.

Here are 3 reasons why we get strokes.

Reason 1: Blocked arteries

In the same way that blocked arteries can result in a heart attack, they can also result in a stroke. If the brain does not get enough blood supply, then in essence it goes into shutdown mode. This can result in mini-strokes, which can usually be successfully treated with medication, or as already indicated it can lead to instant death.

Reason 2: Bad lifestyle

Stress, not taking enough exercise and eating a poor diet are all contributing factors to stroke. However, don't despair, even if you are the world's worst stress head and currently live off double cheeseburgers and beer, then by making changes to your diet you can decrease your risk of stroke significantly. The good news is that you don't even have to make the changes all in one go, which a lot of people find impossible to do. Simply making small changes on a weekly or monthly basis can totally alter your destiny.

Reason 3: Underlying medical conditions

Underlying medical conditions for example, having high blood pressure can significantly increase your chances of getting a stroke. You should have your blood pressure taken on a regular basis. You can even buy a kit from your drugstore to enable you to do this at home. If your blood pressure is high, then there is medication that you can take to get it back down to a normal level.

Understanding the risk factors, and then acting upon them is a key factor in reducing the likelihood of you suffering a stroke. It is far better that you take action now, before it is too late.

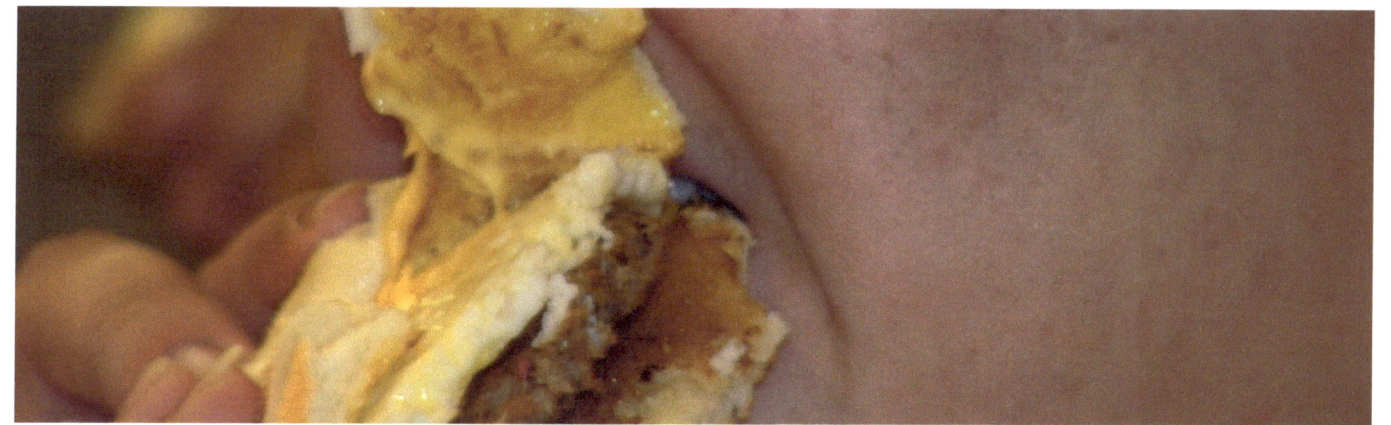

3 Reasons Why people get fat

Regardless of your height and weight, it is very easy to have an opinion as to whether someone else is too fat or too thin. While images of obese people send the media into a frenzy and results in a lot of finger-pointing and name calling, on the flipside size zero models have also come under intense scrutiny recently. So how as a civilized society, do we achieve the right balance? One person's fat might be someone else's cuddly. So, while there are probably dozens of reasons; some more finely nuanced than others, here are 3 reasons why people get fat.

Reason 1: They eat too much

Okay, so this isn't exactly rocket science. However, if you eat more calories than you burn off then you are going to put on weight. While a soup or salad might not be everyone's taste when it comes to lunch, filling your face with burgers and pizza on a daily basis isn't going to help your cause. While depriving yourself of the foods that you love will inevitably lead to you over-indulging, the key as with most things in life is in moderation.

Reason 2: They don't exercise enough

You don't have to become a gym bunny to start getting the exercise that you need. Taking a 30 minute power walk each day can be just as effective. Far too many people cite lack of time as the reason they don't take exercise. Yes, it can be incredibly difficult when you are say working two jobs, and then going home and looking after your baby. However, incorporating exercise into your daily routine can make the world of difference.

Reason 3: They have low self-esteem

Low self-esteem is seriously bad for your health. Not only can it trigger depression, and hold you back from making the advances in your career that you deserve, but it can also lead to over-eating, over-drinking. All of which has a knock on effect on your health.

There are genuine reasons why some people become overweight. However, it doesn't matter what stage in the cycle you are at, simply start making the changes that you need.

3 Reasons Why Grass Fed Beef is better for you

When you eat or buy beef, do you stop to check whether the animals used have been grass fed? Did you even know that grass fed beef is better for you? Well, it is! Here are 3 reasons why grass fed beef is better for you.

Reason 1: Grass fed beef contains the fats your body needs

Not just beef, but all grass fed products, are proven to be better for your health. They are rich in all of the fats that your body requires to keep you healthy, and they are low in the fats that can cause disease. What better reason do you need to start always eating grass fed beef?

Reason 2: Omega 3 and other fats are crucial for good health

Omega 3 fatty acids are vital for good health. They're essential for normal growth and they can prevent and treat such things as: coronary heart disease, arthritis and cancer. Your body cannot make these fats itself, which is why it's important that you have them in your diet. When it comes to meat, the best way of getting omega 3 into your diet this is through eating grass fed products. Omega 6 fats and others are also just as important.

Reason 3: Our ancestors knew best!

Ancestors of human beings perhaps knew better, because they only ate grass fed animals. It's the natural and best way; after all, every cell and system of your body functions better as a result of eating animals that have been raised eating grass.

Still not convinced? Grass fed beef is naturally leaner than grain fed beef. In grain fed beef, omega 3's content is only 1%, whereas it's 7% of the total fat of grass fed beef. The recommended ratio of omega 6 to omega fats is 3:1. Grass fed beef contains the recommended ratio, whilst grain fed beef doesn't.

HOME

3 Reasons Why renting a home is better than buying

To rent or to buy? That is the question that is first and foremost on the minds of millions of young people across the world right now. A direct consequence of the global financial crisis and soaring property prices has resulted in a lot of people being at very least temporarily out-priced out of the housing market. A lot of people also feel peer and parental pressure to buy their own home. But is this necessarily the right move for you? To be honest, it all depends upon your own personal situation, as well as these 3 reasons why renting a home is better than buying.

Reason 1: It gives you greater flexibility

While having a home to call your own can seem like a wonderful thing, it can also be incredibly restrictive. Renting for say six or twelve months means that you are not tied to a mortgage and leaves you the option of going off on your travels at the end of your tenancy. You are only young once and getting shackled with a mortgage too early in your life can have serious implications for your emotional wellbeing.

Reason 2: You can see if your relationship is going to work

While moving in together can be wonderful when everything is going according to plan, it can also be an absolutely horrendous nightmare when things go wrong and you are having to disentangle from each other. Renting gives you the time and the space to concentrate on what is really important: your relationship. A six month tenancy agreement is small changed when compared to a twenty-five year mortgage!

Reason 3: You don't have to worry about repairs

Imagine that it is the middle of winter, all of your cash has gone on the festive celebrations when suddenly your roof springs a leak. If you are renting, then it is not your problem. All you have to do is phone your landlord and have them have someone fix it for you. Repairs and hidden costs can quickly mount up. Renting can help you sleep an awful lot easier.

So, if you are trying to decide what is best for you, make sure that you take some time out to really mull over your options and figure out what it is that you want before making the big leap!

3 Reasons Why buying a home is better than renting

Opinion is pretty evenly divided within both camps as to whether it is better to buy a home or to rent it. For example, those that lean towards renting would argue that they have greater flexibility and freedoms. That they don't have to worry about an unexpected repair bill coming in and derailing their family finances. However, buying your own home is arguably most people's dream. So, in case you still need a little convincing here are 3 reasons why buying a home is better than renting.

Reason 1: You are not wasting money

Many people believe that by paying their hard-earned cash month in and month out to a landlord that they are as good as throwing money down the drain; burning it. By buying a home even with a mortgage you are making a solid investment in your own future. Even if it takes you twenty-five years to achieve your goal, you will one day wind up with a home that you can call your own.

Reason 2: You are building an inheritance for your children

This is arguably one of the primary reasons why home ownership is so desirable. The knowledge that in death you are passing on the family home and safeguarding your children's future is a very comforting one. A lot of families see this as a right and is a huge motivating factor for people attempting to get onto the property market.

Reason 3: You can decorate it however you wish

Whether you favor clean pastels, or want your house to look like a gothic dream. Home ownership is the best way of doing this without landing yourself in hot water with the landlord. While a lot of landlords are happy for you to make modest changes to the interior of their home, they certainly wouldn't want you making any permanent changes.

Made your mind up yet? Buying your own home often depends upon your ability to save a deposit and get a mortgage. Whatever your aspirations, your dream home is surely out there waiting for you.

3 Reasons Why coats and suits can't be washed and need to be pressed

Most people have been in the horrendous situation of needing to go for a job interview, or heaven help us a funeral and discovering that their best coat or suit has a gigantic stain all the way down the front. The horror of that particular situation! However, aside from the inconvenience that this presents there are solid reasons why you can't just pop your suit in the washing machine and then hang it out to try.

Here are 3 reasons why coats and suits can't be washed and need to be pressed.

Reason 1: The heat can ruin your clothes

Depending upon the materials used to make your suit, then they can easily become damaged if you attempt to wash them in a conventional washing machine. Anything that comes directly from an animal's back, such as wool from sheep, cashmere etc. all needs to be treat with kid gloves. Silk will also get ruined if it is washed. So, you need to read your instructions very carefully and follow all advice to the letter.

Reason 2: Delicate stuff might fall off in the wash

This usually applies more to women than men, but say for example you have delicate lace or buttons, then these can easily come off in the wash and is another reason why you will need to have it dry cleaned or pressed

Reason 3: Clothing can lose its shape

Imagine if you have spent several hundred dollars on your suit. Are you really going to run the risk of wrecking its shape just for the sake of putting it in the washing machine? Yes, you may experience every emotional imaginable at the prospect of having to fork out for pressing, but those emotions will be multiplied tenfold if you do the unthinkable.

3 Reasons Why the Housing crises happened in 2008

Sometimes circumstances can collide, making a potentially sticky or bad situation a million times worse. This is precisely what happened in 2008 when the housing crisis, which is frequently also referred to as the US Subprime mortgage crisis happened to collide head on with the global financial crisis that was also building steam. While the economy may well have been able to handle the housing crisis in ordinary circumstances, unfortunately this time it was just a step too far.

Here are 3 reasons why the housing crises happened in 2008.

Reason 1: House prices plummeted

The recession in America started in 2007 and went on until 2009. In the midst of this, house prices fell dramatically which then led to a record number of foreclosures. This of course, ensued in misery for those losing their homes of course, but also misery for the wider economy.

Reason 2: Household debt increased

In addition to mortgage backed securities (MBS) a lot of people had also piled additional pressure on themselves with collateralized debt obligations (CDO) as well as the usual credit cards etc. Unable to sell their homes because of the plummeting house prices they now found themselves trapped in a vicious circle that they were unable to get out of.

Reason 3: The banks and other financial institutions

It is now widely accepted that Wall Street and other financial hubs around the world behaved irresponsibly at this time. Think Lehman Brothers. The reckless disregard for the savings of investors triggered fury around the globe, and fueled anger and distrust in our financial institutions that still lingers today.

RELATIONSHIPS

3 Reasons Why we fall in love

Why do we fall in love? Do you know the answer to that question? It's a difficult one to answer; the main reason being that 'love' is something we can all define differently.

Here are three reasons why we fall in love.

Reason 1: Love is natural

Most people will have been in love at some point in their lives. Many will be in love right at this very moment! But why do we do so? Every creature needs a mate, but falling in love has nothing to do with things associated with reproduction. Though just like many creatures, human beings need to have affection and the warmth of another body. When you couple those natural instincts with our evolution of intelligence and the spawning of things like 'romanticism', you'll get a little closer to our modern day meaning of love.

Reason 2: Attraction and magic

We fall in love because we're attracted to someone. There are plenty of biological, hormonal reasons for being attracted to someone, but surely above and beyond the clinical findings, people are attracted to one another and fall in love with that special someone who feels like they were made especially for you, because… love is magical!

Reason 3: Things like pheromones

The stuffy scientists who don't believe in magic will say that things like pheromones play a part. It could also be due to a subconscious attraction to someone's genes. Believe it or not, when we fall in love, the processes that happen in the brain at the time have similarities to mental illnesses. Do pheromones really make us fall in love?

Maybe it's best to not question why we fall in love. Some things are best experienced without the how's and the why's. When you fall in love, you simply know it, so what else do you need to know?

3 Reasons Why Humans Kiss

Kissing is such a normal part of everyday life that you may have never stopped to ask yourself the question: *why* do humans kiss? Here are three reasons why humans kiss.

Reason 1: The kiss of romance

As you will be only too aware, humans kiss for romantic purposes. It could be argued that it forms part of the courtship ritual; it's that first lip exchange that takes things from friendship and affection to a more romantic or sexual level, so it's an important step in progressing a relationship. Having said that, we're so used to kissing that you may be surprised to learn new studies have shown only around half of human cultures actually kiss in a romantic sense!

Reason 2: Affection

The wider use of kissing, which the majority of cultures do share, is to simply be affectionate. It surely feels like the most natural thing in the world for a parent to kiss their child, or for friends to peck one another on the cheek. Although the styles of kissing may differ from culture to culture (for instance, in some places, men kissing each other on cheeks is the norm, where in others it's not), kissing as a sign of affection seems to be a natural and universal thing. As with a hug, us humans need to be close to our loved ones and display that.

Reason 3: Did our environmental separations cause kissing?

As natural as it seems to kiss, most animals actually don't. You'll be aware of some, like chimpanzees, who do kiss, but humans are certainly amongst the minority when it comes to kissing. So what does set us apart from most of the animal kingdom? Perhaps our kissing behavior only evolved once we somewhat separated ourselves from the natural world. Many ancient tribes have been shown to not kiss, so perhaps our isolation brought us together in new affection giving ways.

Whether it's the kiss of a romantic partner or an affectionate kiss from your daughter, you'll never look at kissing in the same way again.

3 Reasons Why wedding dresses are usually white

Women are very particular when it comes to their wedding dress. That's only normal, because their wedding is one of the most important events they'll ever experience in life. But why is it that wedding dresses are usually white and not of other colors?

Here are three reasons why wedding dresses are usually white.

Reason 1: Blame it on Queen Victoria

Queen Victoria was the trendsetter of white wedding dresses. She wore a lovely plain white wedding gown during her wedding to Prince Albert in 1840. To this day, many brides still follow in her footsteps and wear white on their big day. Contrary to what others may say about the link between white and a woman's virginity, Queen Victoria chose white simply because she liked it.

Reason 2: Cleanliness and luxury

Based on the notes of Hanne Blank, white dresses denote purity and speak of cleanliness and luxury. That's because a white wedding dress is difficult to keep clean, especially in outdoor weddings or at the reception. Many even see it as impractical to wear. Nonetheless, the fact that white is a luxurious color and is readily available makes it a favorite by brides-to-be.

Reason 3: Emblem of purity and innocence of girlhood

Queen Victoria's white wedding dress sparked the interests of many during her time and was an ongoing topic in many newspaper columns. Pure white gowns are also considered the emblem of purity and innocence. When people say purity, it doesn't refer to virginity, but being pure of the heart. This is based on the Godey's Lady's Book released on 1849, which was one of the first American women magazines.

3 Reasons Why we put diamonds on engagement rings

Why are diamonds so often the stones that are set in engagement rings? Have you ever wondered why it's the case? Well, if you are curious to find out, here are 3 reasons.

Reason 1: Diamonds are the very best!

There's nothing that speaks of class, expense and quality like a diamond engagement ring. People choose diamonds because they are simply seen as: the best! Whether it is from exposure through companies like Tiffany's, or Marilyn Monroe's famous song and movie, as a society, diamonds are seen as the top stone to be had. So when it comes to engagement rings, it is obvious to see why many people desire a diamond.

Reason 2: Classy and fashionable

You may be surprised to learn that diamond engagement rings are a fairly recent thing. They only first became popular in the 1930s. They soon became more widely available and by 1965, diamond engagement rings were an absolute must; with 80 percent of all new brides in the United States having them. Not only do people want the best available, they also want what the Jones's have!

Reason 3: It's all down to just one man

People would not wear diamond engagement rings at all if it was not for Archduke Maximillian of Austria, because back in 1477, he commissioned the very first diamond engagement ring. This, naturally, caused the rest of Europe's nobility and aristocracy to want the same.

Of course, plenty of people don't wear diamond engagement rings. Many will not do so because they simply can't afford it. Others will choose a stone that is personal to them (such as a birthstone) or they will simply want a more modest affair. After all, marriage is about love, not money and fashion. Isn't it?

3 Reasons Why we have Valentine's day

When Valentine's Day comes around, and you are racing around for flowers and chocolates at the last minute, do you ever wonder why we have the day in the first place? If you're interested to know, here are 3 reasons why we have Valentine's Day.

Reason 1: The history

Valentine's Day, also known as St. Valentine's Day, is celebrated in many countries all over the world. There are many stories pertaining to St. Valentine himself, who was a Christian saint, and February 14th was a religious feast day associated with him. The association of love and romance being attached to the day didn't come about until the 18th century. It was in Geoffrey Chaucer's circles that the day was used as a celebration of the new courtly love that was evolving at the time. Eventually the day evolved further still; into the day for lovers to express their feelings to their loved ones, and into the modern Valentine's Day where greeting cards, chocolates and flowers are all associated as tokens of that love.

Reason 2: People want it

The evolvement of Valentine's Day into its present day incarnation mostly came about because of the general public. Such things as dates may be able to be attributed to old Christian festivals, but the spirit of Valentine's Day, and the fact that it has been kept alive and flourishes more than ever today, is paramount to human beings' desire to express love. That's why we have Valentine's Day! There *should* be a day to celebrate romantic love!

Reason 3: Commercialization

A more cynical view might say that we have Valentine's Day in its current form due to marketing, but that wouldn't be quite right. As much as the day has been turned into a commercial opportunity, just as with Christmas, Easter and others, that's simply the world that we live in! Just because we live in a commercial world, it doesn't mean that the giving of greetings cards and roses should be diminished in any way. They are symbols of tradition now and are used to express love.

3 Reasons Why people get engaged, before getting married

Why do people get engaged before getting married? Plenty of people still adopt this practice, even though many prefer to just head straight for the wedding!

Here are 3 reasons why people get engaged before getting married.

Reason 1: Origins

It basically comes down to tradition. The origin of getting engaged (in Europe) originally comes from the Jewish book: the Torah. In the first place, this is outlined as marriage consisting of two parts: 'erusin' (meaning sanctification) which is the ceremony of betrothal, and 'nissu'in', the actual marriage ceremony. There is also a process called 'kiddushin' in the Jewish book: the Talmud. This corresponds more closely with today's version of engagement. Similar rituals were later adopted in Ancient Greece, and, in basis, the custom has remained to the present day.

Reason 2: Culture

Engagement is still very popular in some countries, but more in some than others. Its tradition is obviously religious, and often this is still true. Many Christian families believe that it's right to have an engagement before you get married. Although not strictly religious anymore, the act of being engaged can often come down to specific cultural beliefs.

Reason 3: Be romantic

Why not get engaged? You've just proposed, so why not draw it out for a while until you are ready to marry? For many people, they can't afford to get married and will only have a wedding when their circumstances (financial or career, for instance) allow it. By becoming engaged, you have made a public declaration to your love. It is a binding promise that you will get married when the time is right.

Engagement isn't suitable for all. Plenty of people don't want to hang about. You've found the one you love, so why not whisk them off to the church or registry office straight away? Ultimately, whether you yourself get engaged before marriage is simply a choice that's up to you.

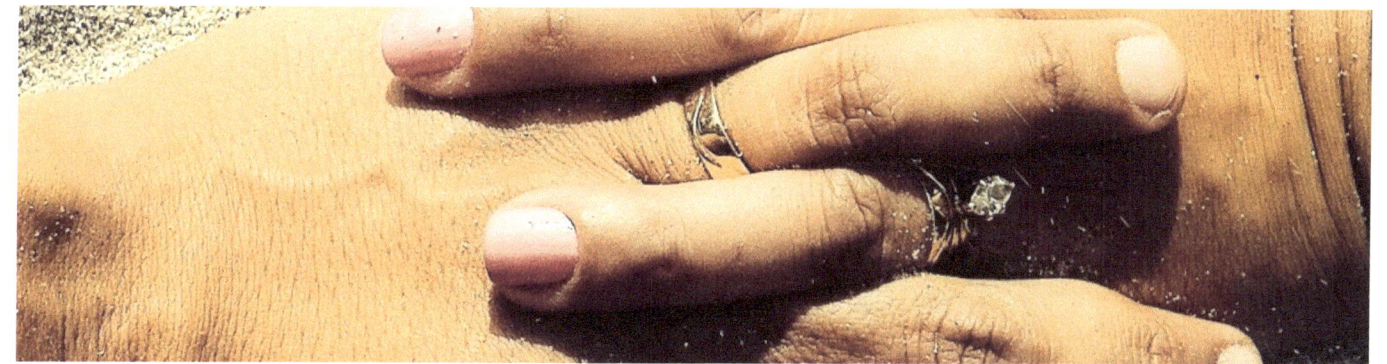

3 Reasons Why men buy women engagement and marriage rings. not the other way around

Have you ever wondered why it is that men are the ones who buy engagement and marriage rings for their future wives, instead of it being round the other way?

Here are 3 reasons why men buy women engagement and marriage rings. not the other way around.

Reason 1: Tradition

Traditionally, it's men who do the asking. Although there is so much flexibility in how one goes about such things in the modern age, and thankfully so, the norm still tends to be that the man asks the woman for her hand in marriage. Gender stereotypes aside, this isn't a bad thing at all. Many like to live by tradition and it adds to the whole romantic nature of the marriage proposal. Plenty of men like to ask and plenty of women like men to ask! So when it comes to buying a ring, the same rules apply. Whilst the tradition of the man getting down on one bended knee and presenting a ring continues to stay alive, men will continue to buy women rings.

Reason 2: Cultural and religious differences

It very much depends on the culture though. For many people, whether for religious reasons or cultural traditions, both the man and the woman will buy each other rings; engagement ones or wedding rings. So it simply depends on how you were brought up and what your own beliefs and views are on the matter at hand (no pun intended).

Reason 3: Romanticism

It's not just rings, but also traditionally, it tends to be the man who buys presents for the woman. In old times this would simply have been due to the male dominated world, where men worked and had money and women were taken care of. As much as these attitudes have changed, and perhaps not enough, there can still be something inherently romantic about the man wishing to look after the love of his life.

What do you think? Would you want your man to buy your engagement or wedding ring? Would you want your woman to buy you the same token? Ultimately, it just comes down to personal choice.

TRAVEL

3 Reasons Why sign posts in US roads and many places around the world are green

If you've ever wondered why road signs in many parts of the world are green, you are not alone. Every road sign seems to have their own unique color, but why? Is it really so random, or is there a science to it?

Here are three reasons why road signs in the US are green.

Reason 1: Green means go

The US Department of Transit has a color coding system. Highway signs and street signs, as well as all informational signs are all green. This includes town sings, street name signs in residential areas. Traditionally, green is more visible to motorists at night time, which is why the green street signs have a reflective quality to them.

Reason 2: Yellow means slow

In 1868, the first crude traffic signals were invented in England and powered by gas. They were two colors, just red (stop) and green (yield). When a gas powered traffic light exploded when a police officer was working on it, they ended up switching the entire city to electric powered traffic lights.

Amber traffic signals were first introduced in 1920 during a chaotic traffic area in Detroit in order to get motor drivers to yield immediately before a stop. Traditionally, yellow signs usually denote a hazard or some sort of cautionary area where we must yield.

Reason 3: Red means stop

In some jurisdictions, such as parts of Texas as well as other small town, the state and county actually have control over the color of street signs. Don't be surprised the next time you're diving around Texas and discover blue or silver street signs! This is determined by the local department of transit as opposed to the federal DOT. While blue signs usually donate rest or gas areas on highways, in certain areas, the local department of transit has authority over what colors the signs are and like to be a little different.

The more you know the more you grow. Thank you for reading about why street signs are certain colors in certain places – now you have some interesting facts to talk about at your next gathering.

3 Reasons Why Las Vegas became the prime destination for gambling and casinos

Las Vegas, Nevada is often billed as the city where you can "see and experience it all." In this article, we will look at how Las Vegas was founded, why it is the destination for gambling and casinos and why you can still "see and experience it all" in Las Vegas.

Here are three reasons why Las Vegas became the prime destination for gambling and casinos.

Reason 1: Las Vegas is an oasis

The city of Las Vegas was "discovered" around 1830 by Rafael Rivers, when he stumbled upon what is now known as Las Vegas Springs, an oasis in the desert which may have saved the lives of him and his caravan. 14 years later, John C. Fremont led an expedition and camped at Las Vegas Springs. Although the word "Las Vegas" translates to "The Meadows" in Spanish, the city is famous for its oasis-like presence in an otherwise deadly valley of desert. As for the now famous Las Vegas oasis springs stretching across Death Valley and into California, they were the sole reasons traders were able to travel across the barren desert and colonize California, making it what it is today.

Reason 2: Las Vegas is a waypoint

Around 1890, when railroad developers decided to camp in the water-rich city of Las Vegas, paved streets, saloons and hotels started to pop-up, the first of which was Jackie Gaughan's Plaza Hotel located at Main and Fremont in what is now Downtown Las Vegas. When large lots of property were auctioned off in Las Vegas, casinos went up in nearly all of them. Today, the city of Las Vegas is still a waypoint for travelers from all over the world who enjoy casinos.

Reason 3: Las Vegas was the first

Nevada was the first state in the US to legalize gambling. Although gambling was briefly outlawed in Las Vegas on October 1st, 1910, Las Vegas residents quickly took to illegal, underground gambling until 1931, when the state of Nevada legalized gambling once again in a bill passed in order to tax casinos and fund Las Vegas public schools.

Because of the reasons above, it is clear that, although Nevada was the first state to legalize gambling, the last state to make gambling illegal, and the first state to re-legalize gambling, Las Vegas will continue to be the best and only destination for those who wish to gamble legally at casinos.

3 Reasons Why the pyramids were built

Have you ever wondered why the pyramids were built? Well, there is not that straightforward a question to answer. Plenty of people have different views on the topic, so it's something that should most certainly be looked into in more detail if the subject takes your fancy. Why were those magnificent, ancient structures built?

Here are three reasons why the pyramids were built.

Reason 1: The official answer

Ask any Egyptologist (well, most) and they'll tell you that the Egyptian pyramids on the Giza plateau were tombs. It is assumed that Pharaoh Cheops constructed the Great Pyramid to be his burial chamber. Only, doubt may be cast because actually no bodies were ever found in any of these pyramids. Even in the time of the looters, when they blasted open the Great Pyramid, there was no suggestion that mummies had ever been found. So, was the Great Pyramid just a burial chamber with a missing body, or was it something else?

Reason 2: New discoveries

In the early 1990s, Robert Bauval published a book which threw new light on the purpose of the pyramids. He discovered that the three pyramids of Giza lined up exactly in accordance with the three stars of Orion's Belt. On further investigation, the accuracy was uncanny and it was soon apparent that other things also mirrored the heavens, such as the Nile's position next to the pyramids being in accordance with the Milky Way's position to Orion. When you also find out that there are two shafts in the so-called King's Chamber which point to Alpha Draconis and Orion, not to mention plenty of facts like the numerology of pi being contained in the Great Pyramid's measurements, you might begin to see that at the very least, these pyramids were not solely tombs.

Reason 3: Many mysterious theories

Others have more outlandish theories. Search the internet and you will see claims for aliens having constructed the pyramids or the King's Chamber being a sort of trans-dimensional-transporter type thing! Plenty of people also believe that there are spiritual secrets contained in the pyramids.

Or maybe it's just simpler than that. Maybe it's akin to asking, many thousands of dystopian years from now, "Why did they build the Eiffel Tower? And how?"

3 Reasons Why Knowledge is Essential

What do we stand to gain by knowing things? Take a look at some of the most successful people throughout history for the answer to that question: Abraham Lincoln, Henry Ford, Steve Jobs, Maya Angelou, Steven King and the list goes on. They all succeeded at their craft because they were highly knowledgeable in their field, as well as in life.

Knowledge is essential to success. It's a key component that drives people to succeed because the more knowledgeable an individual is, the more difficult it becomes to sit idly by and not put that knowledge into action. Knowledge often begets action. This is why having an educated community is essential to the improvement of any society. It all starts by picking up a book. Reading is a window into other worlds which allows people to gain essential knowledge, vicarious experience, imagination, creativity and much more.

Here are three reasons why knowledge is essential.

Reason 1: Knowledge is power

Never forget that true power stems, not just from *knowing* things, but the way in which we utilize that knowledge. Conversely, ask yourself, what becomes of the uninformed individual? He is powerless to change his situation. Information is the cornerstone of change in both individuals and in society, and only by *knowing* things will we gain the power to change things.

How will you use your power of knowledge? At 3 Reasons Why, we believe in using knowledge to empower people everywhere. That's why we're hosting a series of events with knowledgeable guest speakers. Find the next 3RW event near you at events.3reasonswhy.com.

Reason 2: Knowledge is infectious

Have you ever learned something that you just had to share with another person? Knowledge is a fire that burns within us, begging to be released and spread from one person to the next. That is our mission here at 3RW – to spread knowledge to as many people as possible on as many topics as possible. Visit www.3ReasonsWhy.com and start spreading more knowledge today.

Reason 3: Knowledge is the remedy

Knowledge is the cure to poverty, because informed individual has an endless array of skills at his disposal which he uses to earn his keep. Knowledge is the cure to violence because the informed individual knows that there are alternative ways in which a conflict can be resolved. Knowledge is the cure to hunger, because the informed individual is resourceful and can find sustenance even in the harshest conditions. Knowledge is the remedy to most of life's little problems.

The world we live in is constantly in flux with an endless ebb and flow of information, all of which are made up of reasons that are ripe for *knowing*. As you walk down the crossroad of life, striving endlessly towards knowledge, there will undoubtedly be plenty of noise along the way. It can be easy to get distracted by the noise, but it is the task of every knowledge seeker to do their best to ignore that noise and find 3 simple reasons for everything.

Thank you for reading *The 3 Reasons Why Book of Lifestyle*. If you enjoyed this book, you can find more reasons for just about everything at www.3ReasonsWhy.com. You can find more books like these available at books.3reasonswhy.com.

Go forth and spread knowledge to the world.